I0211681

Denise and Terry Atkins

———⌘———

You cannot base an entire story on just one chapter.

~Create Happiness Today~

A

BETTER YOU

IN

45 DAYS

Denise and Terry Atkins

©2024 - All Rights Reserved

Denise and Terry Atkins

At the time of this initial publication the links and websites mentioned were active. Atkins Ventures should not be deemed to endorse or recommend any website other than its own, or any content available on the internet. Including, but not limited to any site, blog, or information page not created by Atkins Ventures.

Copyright ©2024 by Denise Atkins | Atkins Ventures

Authors: Denise Atkins and Terry Atkins

All Rights Reserved

ISBN: 978-1-7380110-1-8

Category: Literary

Subject: Self Improvement

First Edition

Published by Heritage Branch

Library and Archives Canada | Government of Canada

https://library/archives.canada.ca

isbn@bac-lac.gc.ca | Tel: 819-994-6872 or 1-866-578-7777

Cover Graphic designed by Terry and Denise Atkins | Atkins Ventures

Denise and Terry Atkins

For Marley

CONTENTS

PREFACE

This book is written with heart-felt thanks to those who helped us along our journey.

To the family and friends who stood with us in the darkness and held the light for us to see, we appreciate you. We cannot name all of you but thank you for reaching out your hand and never turning your back on us. You gave mercy when necessary and kindness when needed.

To our beloved children and their families who faced each twilight beside us, we are eternally grateful. You helped us stand when we fell and speak when we had no words. We love you more than we could possibly express.

To the God we believe in, we forever love you. You gave us hope when we were lost, and a life we never thought we would have together.

All of you helped us realize who we want to be.

To the critics who stood far off and watched as we struggled, we acknowledge you as well. You showed us how to be strong by trying to make us weak. Your harsh words toughened our skin and hardened our resolve. Your lack of care taught us self-reliance and your criticism inspired us to fight even harder for success. We would have never known what love was without you showing us what it was not. We forgive you because forgiveness sets us free.

More than anything, you made us realize who we never want to be.

The Authors

INTRODUCTION

I.

Life can be hard.

This is a truth you already know. We are not trying to discourage you, but to let you know we understand. Everyone's life, no matter how "good", can have tough times. Think about the troubles you endured or are currently battling. What are you facing right now that is causing you to stay up at night? Perhaps it is financial hardships, relationship problems, health issues, or any number of daily challenges. We all have our demons to slay. The question is, "How do we learn to fight?"

Some people might tell you to simply stay positive and things will work themselves out. Others may say life is not fair, so just grow up. The list of platitudes is endless. These voices, while meant to encourage, can make matters worse and leave you feeling as if no one understands your unique challenges. Our goal is to add our voice to your narrative, but not in a diminishing or minimizing way.

We did not write this book from a spectator's perspective concerning how to overcome the dark times life can bring. Rather it is written from the center of the arena and the middle of the fight. We are not strangers to life's ups and downs but learned to enjoy the ride. Here are glimpses of our stories.

Denise grew up in a tight-knit and loving family with her older sister. Even though she was surrounded by caring and attentive parents, as a young girl, she was often ridiculed by extended family members. Their degrading and demeaning comments left her feeling ugly and inadequate. After many years of hearing these negative messages, the care-free little girl she wanted to be was gradually replaced by a self-conscious and insecure teenager. The verbal abuse affected her deep into her adult years

and created a false narrative that she would battle for decades. Sadly, this was just the beginning of her tragedies.

In her late teens, Denise suffered the loss of her beloved maternal grandmother to colon cancer. This created a huge hole in her life. As one of the few positive voices she knew, the absence of her grandma was earth-shattering. Denise had even more loss when her loving mother, (and best friend), died of breast cancer after a 10-year battle. The encouragement and support of these two women were cornerstones in Denise's life and she felt adrift without them.

Somewhere between the deaths of her grandmother and mother, her first marriage ended in an unexpected divorce. This left Denise devastated, bearing the stigma of being an unemployed single parent in the 90's. She eventually found work but endured such horrific sexual and emotional harassment from her employer that she was forced to quit the job. The scars from the workplace abuse further destroyed her self-image and worth, but Denise pressed on for the sake of her young son.

In time she remarried and began rebuilding her life launching several businesses with her new husband. But many years later, Denise's challenges would continue. She faced the loss of her fun-loving and caring father to heart disease. Then the life-altering death of her second husband of 25 years after an 8-year battle with thyroid cancer. The list of hardships and tragedies could go on including the loss of an unborn child, her own health concerns, and much more.

However, Denise does not consider herself a victim or somehow special because she suffered hard times. Instead, she looks at the adversities of her life as lessons that taught her to be strong. Like her father, she has a quick wit and insatiable zest for life. Like her grandmother and mother before her, she is a fighter who loves unconditionally.

If you were to meet Denise, you would see that she is simply a person who refuses to let negative experiences define who she is. She does not let anything hold her back from getting the most out of life. Instead of allowing her dark days to consume her, Denise chooses to use what she has been through to help others find joy amid their trials. One of her greatest dreams is to be a light in the darkness of others and give them a smile that is sometimes hard to find.

Terry had his own personal strife growing up. As a child of divorce, with little to no contact with his father, Terry felt that he was not good enough to be loved. His mother worked numerous jobs as a single parent to provide for him and his younger brother. Due to her work schedule, Terry spent much of his life alone or caring for himself and his sibling. This meant that many of the household responsibilities landed on his shoulders, and he was never allowed to just be a kid. He had to grow up quickly, which made him feel responsible for everyone around him. To this day he battles the tendency to put the needs of others ahead of his own, sometimes to a fault.

As an awkward and inquisitive child, Terry had few close friends and was constantly looking for ways to fit in. His teachers often told him that he possessed tremendous potential but lacked focus. These messages, along with abandonment from his father, greatly impacted his self-esteem in a negative way. Throughout the years he became withdrawn and timid, never really understanding his place in the world or his true value.

Eventually, Terry grew up and joined the military, married, and raised four children. The 29-year marriage was tumultuous, and neither partner was their best self. He was determined not to repeat the abandonment that his father inflicted, so he committed to the relationship for the sake of his kids. Once the children were grown, (and started families of their own), Terry filed for divorce. This decision led to three of his adult children choosing to remove themselves from his life along with their families.

Abandonment and estrangement have been a constant theme in Terry's life, but miraculously he still has the capacity to love and build quality relationships. Somehow, he still greets every day with gladness, and believes that there is always a light in even the deepest darkness.

Denise and Terry Atkins

———————◦⚮◦———————

Those who know him see his broad smile, calm demeaner, and infectious sense of humor. Most do not know the mountains he had to climb or the scars of loneliness he carries in his heart. Like Denise, he is a warrior who chooses to use the hurt that life has thrown his way to comfort those who are hurting. He is determined to show that true love always wins out in the end.

———————◦⚮◦———————

However, our story does not end in tragedy. In fact, it is still being written. We were high school friends who miraculously came together after decades, while weathering our individual storms. We reconnected on social media and our friendship picked up where it ended some 30 plus years before.

We spent hundreds of hours on the phone, video chat, and social media building a renewed relationship filled with laughter, tears, and heart-felt communication. Day after day, we grew to know and care for one another deeply. We soon realized that God brought us together to help heal the wounds of our pasts. Terry came to Canada for a visit and we both felt a connection much deeper than mere friendship. We were in love.

Thankfully, our faith in God and love never faltered. Though many thought us foolish, we held firm to the belief that love would find us no matter what came our way. We were married in 2019 and our incredible journey began as husband and wife. Little did we know that every twist and turn was bringing us to this very moment… a moment we are happy to share with you.

II.

The book you hold in your hands is a work built on love through much pain endured. As we established, our lives gave us experience with various challenges. But we understand experience alone does not qualify us to write this book. To offer the best help possible, we completed the following certifications regarding emotional health and wellness:

———————∞———————

Denise is a certified Life Happiness Coach and holds a separate certification in Cognitive-Behavioral Therapy, (CBT). Terry is a certified Meditation and Wellness Coach who also holds a CBT Certificate. Additionally, both of us completed a Life Coaching Masterclass with a focus on client engagement and support.

Together we created a wellness platform called, "Create Happiness Today" (CHT), *www.createhappinesstoday.com.* Our focus is on helping you to live better, love deeper, and laugh more often. We strive to bring healing to heartbroken people through sharing our own life experiences. We strongly believe that by changing your perspective, you can change your life.

*See the **CHT Promo and Coupon Page - page 204**, for details about this worthwhile project.*

We are not speaking as authorities or clinicians regarding mental health and recovery. This book is not a substitute for professional help. If you need in-depth therapy or care, please contact a local healthcare professional or emergency services.

We are also not attempting to "fix" you but are offering a guide to help navigate any dark places in your life. We believe that our unique perspectives on living will be beneficial as you work on yourself. We want your time with us to help open your eyes to a happier you. If you want to live a little better and stand a little taller, then this book is for you.

III.

If you read to this point, then you have already taken a major move toward becoming a greater version of yourself. The world is filled with people who want change, but never do the work required. Familiarity and comfort can make you feel unwilling to shake things up. Fear and doubt can paralyze you and cause you to procrastinate while remaining in the same situation. You may dream of being different, but the shadow of failure can keep you from trying. We commend you on making this decision to dedicate the next forty-five days to your future. That choice alone is why you should succeed.

Each day you will be greeted with one of our custom daily inspirations featured on our CHT social media platforms. The day's entry will include a well-known quote along with a story or article related to the message. At the end of each write-up, you will be prompted with a "Reflection of the Day" and "Daily Affirmation". These are designed to inspire both mindful introspection and practical action regarding the topic at hand. Lastly, there are note-taking sections for you to track your thoughts and progress. These will be extremely valuable as you navigate the pages because they allow you to look back on your growth.

We believe that you will find the day-to-day content to be beneficial, educational, and enlightening. Some writings are general in nature, some are stories of greatness, while others are more personal entries from us. Our hope is that every chapter will encourage you to look inside yourself as you examine your heart and motives. Do your best not to criticize or amplify your faults, but to strengthen your belief that success is possible.

Please do not treat this book like a personal checklist or make it another burdensome chore added to your day. Although it is structured for a forty-five-day cycle, take the time you need to dive deeply into each page. Some topics, such as forgiveness or releasing your past, may take days to complete. That is ok. Success and progress are not measured by the time it takes to complete the book, but how different you are at the end.

Once you complete the forty-five days of reflections and journaling exercises, you should feel more empowered and see yourself in a new light. Your level of confidence in your own abilities should be improved and the negative voices of doubt and discouragement greatly diminished. The goal here is progress, not perfection.

Forty-five days is not nearly enough time to address every area of concern in your life. There will be topics that we do not cover that are

specific to you. In contrast, there may be subjects discussed that have no real bearing on your current situation. Our hope is that most entries hit close to your heart and help you feel less alone.

Remember that inside every one of us lies a broken person who is learning to live through the storms of life. We all go through moments of weakness and insecurity. By making the decision to put one foot in front of the other you are setting yourself apart. Embracing your individual imperfections can help you be honest about the person you were, are, and will be. No one is perfect and that includes you.

By facing your own problems and no longer ignoring them, you can begin to live happier and more fulfilled. This does not mean you will never go through hard times or major difficulties again. But when those moments do come, you may be better equipped to handle and overcome them more easily.

We wish you the very best on your path and are proud of you for taking a major stride toward healing and wellness. Thank you for letting us be a part of your life for the next forty-five days.

~Denise and Terry~

Do what you need to do to be what you want to be.

~Create Happiness Today~

Do what you need to do
to be what you want to be.

Create Happiness Today
www.createhappinesstoday.com
contact@createhappinesstoday.com
#createhappinesstoday

___DO YOU WANT TO BE BETTER?___   *~ DAY 1 ~*

Do you want to be better, or do you just want the bad stuff to go away?

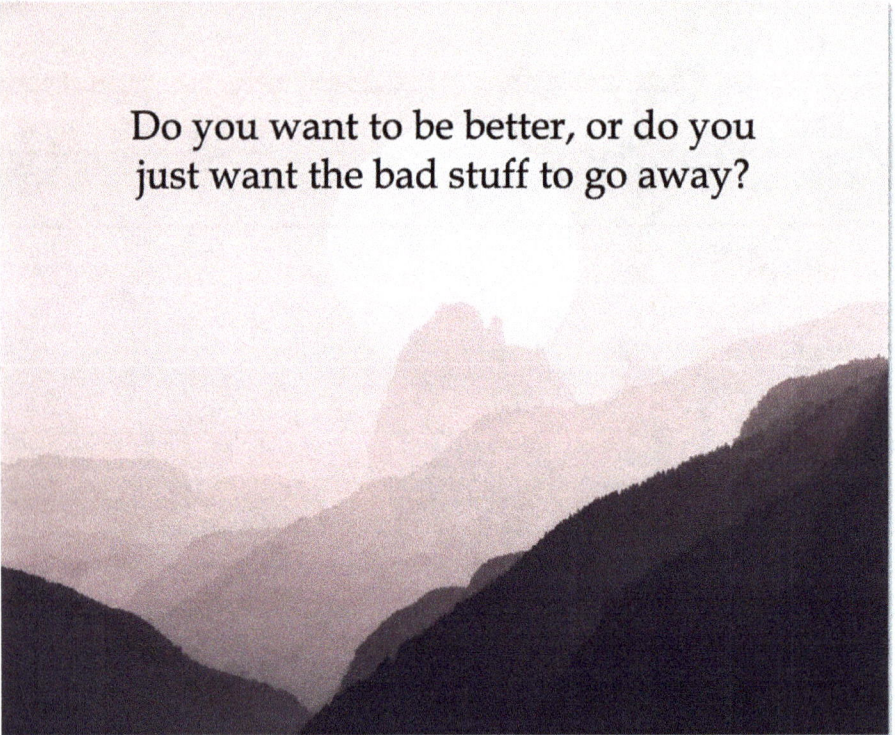

Do you want to be better, or do you just want the bad stuff to go away?

Do the best you can until you know better. Then when you know better, do better.

Maya Angelou

In life, we often find ourselves at crossroads, faced with situations that push us to ask a fundamental question: Do we want to be better, or do we simply want the bad stuff to go away?

To merely wish for the "bad stuff" to disappear is to seek temporary relief, a quick fix to alleviate discomfort. It is to yearn for a bandage solution that covers the wounds but does not address the underlying causes. We end up sticking our heads in the sand or wearing rose-colored glasses thus ignoring our flaws. While understandable, this mindset keeps us stuck in a cycle of stagnation, where we are merely surviving instead of thriving.

On the other hand, desiring to move ahead is a courageous choice. It requires us to confront our weaknesses and see our shortcomings. When we look for ways to alter our thinking or lifestyle, we can view setbacks as valuable lessons. This perspective propels us forward and inspires us to mature emotionally.

Choosing to be different involves making intentional choices, setting goals, and adopting new habits that align with our morals and aspirations. It means investing time and effort in personal development, seeking guidance and support when needed, and being open to feedback and constructive criticism. It is not easy, but it is necessary to become our best selves.

As you stand at this crossroads, ask yourself: Do you want to be better, or do you just want the bad stuff to go away? Step out of your comfort zone, push away your fears, and develop an attitude of continuous improvement.

Remember, the choice is yours, and the goal of fulfilled living is within your reach. Accept it and watch as you evolve into the best version of yourself.

Reflection for Today: How committed are you to making life-long changes? Write down a few areas where you want to see improvement.

Today's Affirmation: I will focus on what I need to work on within myself instead of worrying over what I cannot control. In doing so, I ensure that I will grow from the difficulties I encounter and not simply wish them away.

NOTES:

IT'S ABOUT PROGRESS   *~ DAY 2 ~*

It's more about progress than perfection.

Perfectionism is the enemy of progress.

Winston Churchill

Perfectionism often holds us back from taking action and pursuing our goals. The pursuit of "perfection" can be paralyzing. We can become consumed with the fear of making mistakes and falling short of our own impossibly high standards. How would our lives be different if we challenged the notion of perfection? What if we continually remind ourselves that progress is far more important than attaining an unattainable ideal?

Focusing on progress allows us to celebrate victories and milestones along the way. Rather than being discouraged by setbacks or limitations, we should view them as opportunities to learn. If we are making progress, we are moving forward.

Embracing progress over perfection also helps us acknowledge that living differently is not simple and that trials are inevitable. Everything we have been taught to do began with a struggle. Whether it is learning to walk, talk, or write for the first time, we all went through a period of stumbling through the process. We should keep this same mindset with anything that we pursue in life.

By shifting our focus to progress, we free ourselves from the suffocating pressure of perfectionism. We allow ourselves to take risks, make bad choices, and learn from them. This fosters emphasis on continuous improvement rather than an unrealistic fixed end goal.

Remember that life is a pathway of progress, not a destination of perfection. This truth can turn obstacles into steppingstones and the weight of opposition can strengthen our will. This encourages us to celebrate the small wins and accomplishments.

By prioritizing progress over perfection, we limit discouragement and can see more clearly how far we have come. We are not in competition with anyone else regarding improving our lives, not even ourselves.

Reflection for Today: Do you seek perfection in what you do before feeling successful? Give a recent example.

Today's Affirmation: I release the pressure of striving for flawless outcomes and will focus on improvement. I celebrate the small victories and milestones along the way. I understand that progress forward, no matter how small, is in the right direction.

NOTES:

THE SUM OF YOUR MISTAKES ~ DAY 3 ~

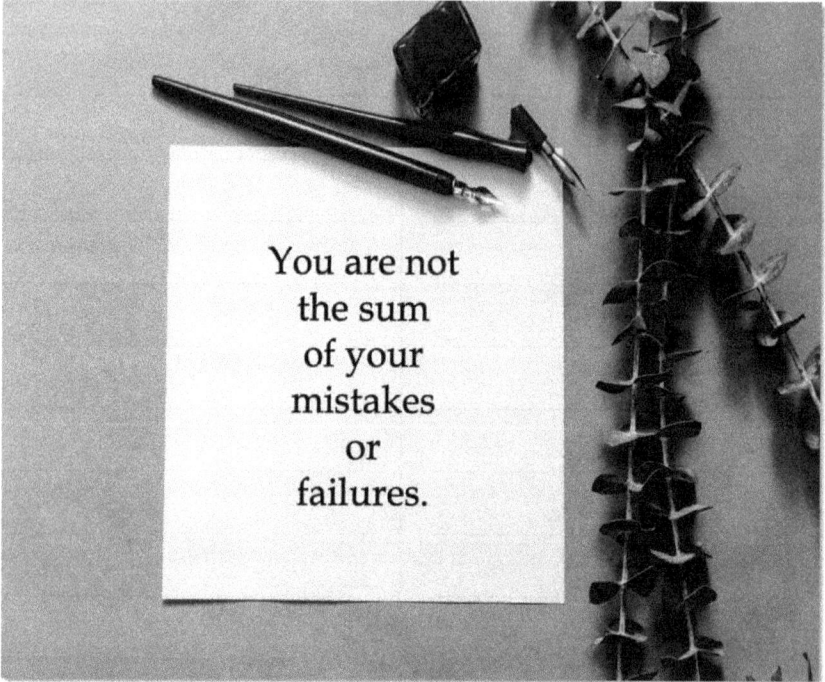

You are not
the sum
of your
mistakes
or
failures.

You are not the sum of your mistakes or failures.

What is done cannot be undone, but at least one can keep it from happening again.

Anne Frank

Read that again... *"You are not the sum of your mistakes or failures"*. Say it out loud as many times as you need to hear it until it sinks in.

No one on this earth is perfect. We all blunder and will fail at something at least once in our lifetime. It is important to realize this and take personal responsibility.

Robert Downey Jr. is a perfect example. As an American actor with immense talent, his internal conflicts led to a decline in his popularity and limited his opportunities in the entertainment industry.

Downey's battle with addiction and legal troubles reached a breaking point in the late 1990s and early 2000s. He had multiple arrests and was in and out of rehab. These served as wake-up moments that caused him to turn his life around.

After getting sober, Downey made a remarkable comeback, both personally and professionally. He landed the iconic role of Tony Stark/Iron Man in the Marvel Cinematic Universe. This catapulted him to global fame and reestablished his reputation as one of Hollywood's most talented actors.

Off-screen, Downey has been an advocate for mental health and has used his platform and notoriety to raise awareness about addiction and the importance of seeking help. He co-founded the production company Team Downey, which focuses on creating projects that promote social and environmental causes.

Robert Downey Jr.'s journey from failures to becoming a beloved actor showcases his ability to overcome adversity. His positive platform serves as an inspiration to others with similar tests and demonstrates the power of second chances.

Like Downey's example, the errors in your life do not define you. The fact that you overcame them should not be ignored. Instead of carrying their weight, use them as a banner for others to follow.

Reflection for Today: What are some of your biggest mistakes in life? Describe one that comes to mind.

Today's Affirmation: I am not defined by my past, but by my ability to rise above it. I release myself from the shadows of my failures. I will learn from my missteps and use them to guide me to a more satisfying life.

NOTES:

A Better You in 45 Days

LET GO   ~ DAY 4 ~

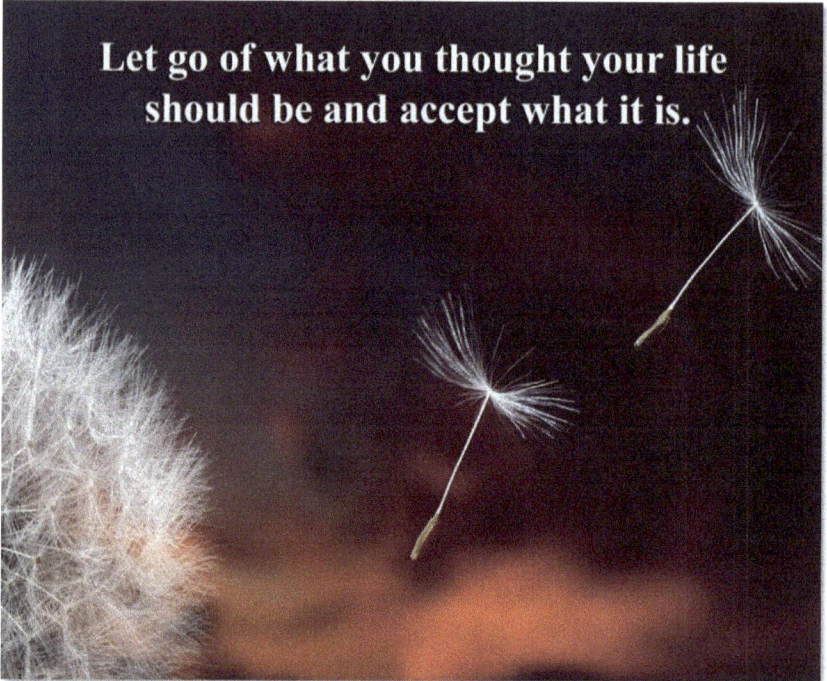

Let go of what you thought your life should be and accept what it is.

Let go of what you thought your life should be and accept what it is.

My happiness grows in direct proportion to my acceptance,

and in inverse proportion to my expectations.

Michael J. Fox

How can you find happiness and contentment when your life does not align with your expectations of how things should be? You often hold onto a dream of what life should look like and are dissatisfied when reality does not agree.

However, there is incredible power in learning to let go of how you thought your life would turn out and accept what your life truly is. It is in this acceptance that you find freedom, peace, and the opportunity for genuine happiness.

Acceptance does not mean giving up on dreams or settling for less. It means acknowledging the reality of your circumstances and making the best of what you have. It means embracing the imperfections, detours, and unexpected twists that life throws your way and releasing the false control you imagine.

Your losses can push you in a direction contrary to what you expected. However, that new direction does not have to be considered a negative outcome. You have no idea how your life would have been impacted if things had "worked out" the way you dreamed.

Those "if only" outcomes you pine over may have led to even greater heartbreak or sadness. There is no way to know, but what you do know is what your life is like at this moment, in this reality.

In addition, wishing you possessed someone else's reality is just as harmful. You do not know the hidden battles others have in their day-to-day lives, but only see the outward side of their existence. They might be worse off than you.

By accepting the truth of your current situation, you can be grateful for the now and accept the present, rather than constantly pursuing an idealized future, or regretting the past.

Learn to let go of what could or should have been. Decide to witness the beauty of the present, the lessons of the past, and the possibilities of the future.

Reflection for Today: List three ways your life has not turned out the way you thought it would.

Today's Affirmation: I let go of any lingering attachments to how things should have been and accept the present moment with open arms. I release any resistance and surrender to the flow of life. I know doing this will guide me towards my highest good.

NOTES:

<u>STAY AMAZED</u>   **<u>~ DAY 5 ~</u>**

Live a life where the little things still amaze you.

The more I live, the more I learn.

The more I learn, the more I realize how much I don't know.

Albert Einstein

I began my long commute home from a difficult day at work when something extraordinary happened. It rained earlier that afternoon, and as I turned onto the main highway, I was greeted by an incredible sight in the sky above. A huge unbroken double rainbow reached from one end of the horizon to the other, (as you can see in the actual photo on the opposite page).

This rare sight was perfect and breathtaking.

I pulled over, took several pictures, and called my husband to share the experience right away because I did not want him to miss it. With me on the phone, he went to the front porch and witnessed the rainbows as well. We spent several minutes admiring the sight and tearfully appreciating its beauty. After a time, we hung up and I got back into my car to continue the drive home.

It was then that I noticed how many people were simply driving by and going about their business with no recognition of what was happening just above them. My heart grew heavy, and I found myself in tears. Not just because of the beauty of what God showed me, but also because it was discarded by so many.

When we are children everything in the world is amazing to us. We see through innocent eyes at the wonder all around. Nature is filled with mysteries and our hearts are eager to find them. But, somewhere along the way the miraculous becomes mundane.

Maybe the disappointments of life or the day-to-day stresses of adulting steal away the splendor of living. Perhaps, in our busyness, we feel like there is nothing left to learn about the world. Whatever the reason, there seems to be a point where most of us begin taking everything for granted. We forget to stop and take notice of the miracles we are surrounded by.

Looking back, I am thankful for the trials I overcame that helped open my eyes to the smallest things in life. I now realize that the small things can be very big things and no matter what I am doing, I should take a moment to look up.

I am so very grateful to have seen those rainbows that day and the memory of sharing them with my husband will stay with me forever. But it saddens me to think of how many people either did not see or did not care about them like I did. They missed a life-changing opportunity to see something spectacular.

You are surrounded by miracles every single day. Remember to take the time to let life still be amazing. Otherwise, you might miss something that takes your breath away.

~Denise~

Reflection for Today: In the notes section, write about something incredible that you may have overlooked today.

Today's Affirmation: I will not let the miraculous become mundane or let my heart believe that I know everything. I will keep my mind and eyes open remembering to look up.

NOTES:

<u>**THE RIGHT PEOPLE**</u>　　　　　*~ DAY 6 ~*

Surround yourself with people who add to your happiness.

Surround yourself with people who add to your happiness.

Surround yourself with those who believe in your dreams,

support your ambitions and bring out the best in you.

Roy T. Bennett

We often underestimate the profound influence our relationships have on our overall well-being and happiness. The people we surround ourselves with can either uplift us or drain our energy. That is why it is crucial to consciously choose to be in the company of those who make us genuinely happy.

When we are in the presence of these types of people, something healthy occurs within us. Their positive energy radiates into our lives, creating a ripple effect that enhances our own sense of contentment. These individuals are like rays of sunshine on a cloudy day, reminding us that beauty exists even during life's greatest trials.

Having supportive and uplifting relationships can also inspire us. We are encouraged to dream bigger, take risks, and chase our passions without fear or judgement. These people see our potential and provide support to help us reach our goals.

Being surrounded by happy energy fosters a sense of belonging and connection. It creates a safe space where we can freely express ourselves, share our joys and sorrows, and find solace in times of need. These relationships become the pillars of our support system, offering comfort and guidance during life's ebbs and flows.

Also, by becoming a happy person, we create opportunities to lift others. This gives our life even more meaning and helps to boost our worth. We enjoy a feeling of accomplishment and wellness as we give out the joy we have received.

Ultimately, surrounding yourself with those who make you happy is vital for self-care. It is a conscious choice to prioritize your own well-being and create laughter, inspiration, and kindness in your life. Treasure these relationships and understand how rare they are. Having a circle of light in your world can only enhance it.

Reflection for Today: Name someone that you should either add to, or remove from, your life. Record how this will make your life better.

Today's Affirmation: I will create uplifting relationships that feed my soul and ignite my creativity. By surrounding myself with people who make me happy, and giving happiness to others, I can become a source of light for someone else.

NOTES:

WHAT DO YOU EXPECT?   ~ DAY 7 ~

We accept the love and
treatment we think we deserve.
(read that again)

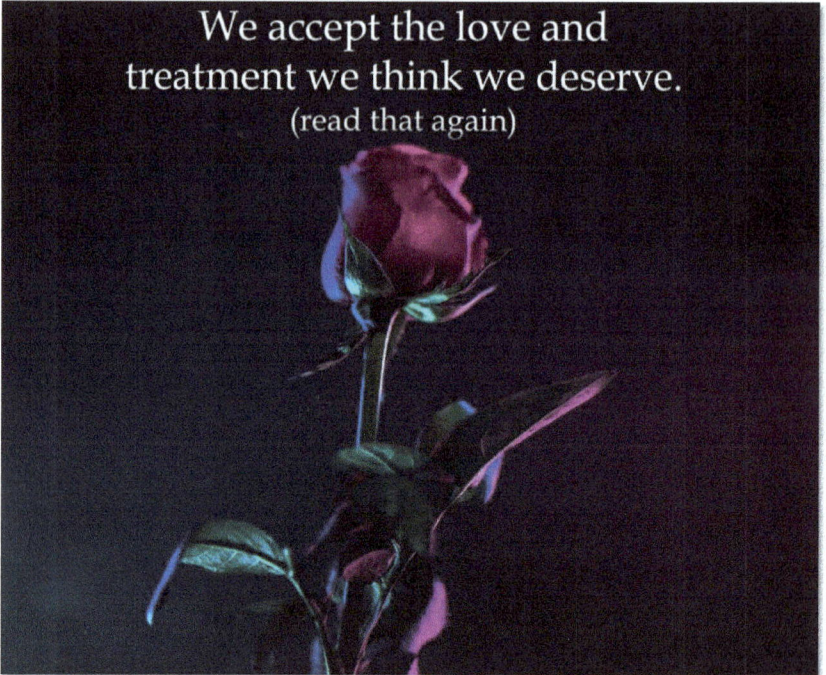

We accept the love and treatment we think we deserve.

You teach people how to treat you by what you allow, what you stop, and what you reinforce.

Tony Gaskins

What do you expect? It is crucial for you to understand the significant role your perception plays in shaping the love and treatment you accept. The truth is the behaviors you attract and tolerate are a direct reflection of your own belief in your worthiness.

When you have a strong sense of worth, you naturally gravitate towards relationships that mirror your standards. You confidently set healthy boundaries, communicate your needs, and select people who genuinely respect, cherish, and uplift you. You deeply understand that you deserve to be loved and treated with utmost kindness and care.

On the other hand, if you encounter feelings of inadequacy, you may find yourself settling for less than you should. You may end up in relationships where you are mistreated, your needs are neglected, or you are diminished because you cannot imagine asking for more. These toxic dynamics only reinforce your negative beliefs about yourself and perpetuate a cycle of unfulfilling relationships.

Breaking free from unhealthy environments requires deep introspection, reflection, and a commitment to respect yourself. This means being willing to walk away from people that do not serve you, regardless of who they are or how difficult it may be. By doing so, you create space for healthier, more fulfilling connections that align with your actual merit.

The behavioral boundaries you enforce regarding the treatment you will tolerate may be hard at first. Fear of conflict, guilt, and emotional attachments may make it difficult for you to stand your ground. Keep this in mind; constantly giving ground may seem like a noble act, but it will eventually create a hole that you will fall into.

You are more valuable than you realize, stronger than you know, and more loved than you can imagine. Never let anyone make you feel otherwise.

Reflection for Today:
Consider a recent situation where you accepted bad behavior from

someone simply to keep the
peace. Write it down.

Today's Affirmation: I
deserve to be treated with dignity
and respect no matter what my
past or present may look like. I
have value and am capable of
setting and upholding boundaries
regarding the type of treatment I
will tolerate.

NOTES:

WHEN THINGS FALL APART ~ *DAY 8* ~

When things seem to be falling apart, they may actually be falling into place.

When things seem to be falling apart, they may actually be falling into place.

Don't be afraid of opposition. Remember, a kite rises against, not with the wind.

Hamilton Wright Mabie

It is very interesting how we often feel overwhelmed by life. But this quote from Hamilton Wright Mabie brings up a great point - we should not be afraid of tough situations because they often lead us to greater heights. He uses the analogy of flying a kite, that rises against the wind, not with it.

Imagine this delicate kite soaring high in the sky, defying gravity. It does not give in to the forces pulling it down; instead, it uses the resistance of the wind to climb even higher. As we live, we come across obstacles that can feel debilitating, but Mabie encourages us to face them head-on.

When we encounter these moments and defeat obstacles, we learn to fly. Just like a kite needs the wind to soar, we can use these tough situations to our advantage.

We can choose an alternate perspective on difficult moments. Instead of fearing or avoiding them, we should see them as opportunities to grow. It is important to understand that opposition and difficulties are a natural part of life. They test our abilities, push us out of our comfort zones, and make us stronger.

Think about it - every great success story has setbacks along the way. Whether a famous athlete, a successful entrepreneur, or an accomplished artist, all had to overcome hurdles to reach their goals. They did not let anything stop them, but instead used adversity as fuel to keep going.

The next time you find yourself in the middle of hardships, do not let them intimidate you. Spread your wings, soar higher, and fly. The only person who can stop you from dreaming is you. Though you may have moments of doubt and weakness, if you persist, you will not fail. The only way to fail is to stop trying.

Reflection for Today: Think of a current circumstance that will bring more joy to your life once you conquer it. Describe how things would be different.

Today's Affirmation: Just like a kite soaring against the wind, I rise higher with every obstacle in my way. I am not afraid to go against the flow, because I know that greatness lies on the other side of opposition. I can conquer anything that comes my way.

NOTES:

A Better You in 45 Days

THE OTHER SIDE OF FEAR   *~ DAY 9 ~*

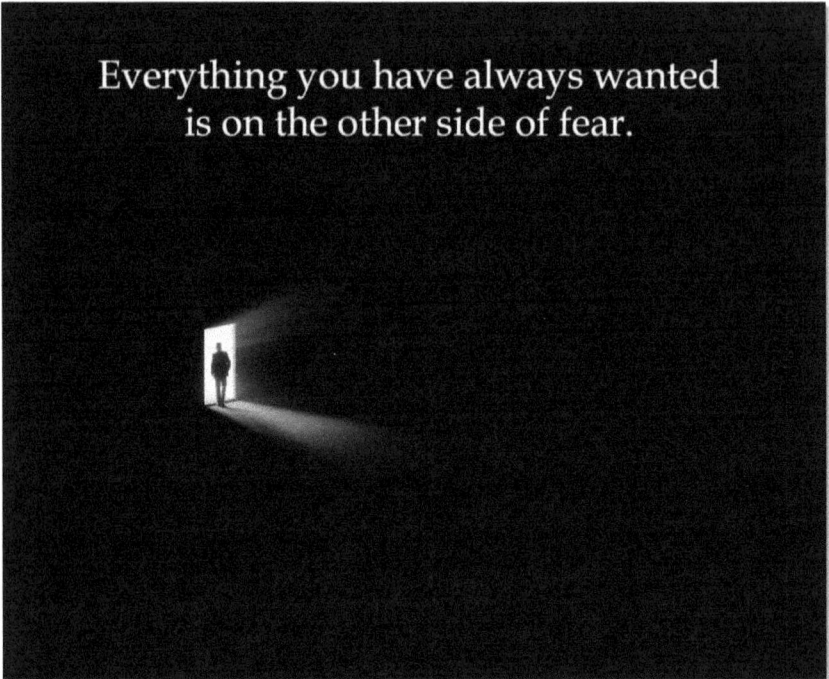

Everything you have always wanted
is on the other side of fear.

Everything you have always wanted is on the other side of fear.

Fear has two meanings:

'Forget Everything and Run' or 'Face Everything and Rise.'

Zig Ziglar

Simone Biles is one of the most remarkable female Olympic athletes of all time. But her road to greatness was not an easy one and could have been derailed many times over by fear.

As a child, Biles had a tumultuous upbringing. Her mother struggled with substance abuse that led to Simone and her siblings being placed in foster care for several years. At the age of six, she was adopted by her grandparents, Ron and Nellie Biles, who eventually introduced her to gymnastics during a daycare field trip.

Simone was immediately drawn to the sport but had an intense fear of heights. Her first steps into the world of gymnastics were daunting. With the encouragement of her coaches and family, she gradually began to confront her fear. Through countless hours of training and repetition, Biles developed the physical and mental ability to perform gravity-defying moves with confidence.

In time, Simone learned to execute her routines with flawless precision, including intricate flips, twists, and acrobatic elements. Her ability to conquer fear of heights allowed her to excel and shine.

In 2013, at the age of 16, she made her debut as a senior competitor and won the all-around title at her first world gymnastics championship. This victory made her the first African American woman to claim the title.

During the 2016 Rio Olympics, she won four gold medals, including the individual all-around, vault, and floor exercise, as well as a team gold medal. Her exceptional performances showcased her incredible skills, power, and precision. This solidified her status as one of the greatest gymnasts of all time.

Simone Biles has won a total of 19 world championship medals, making her the most decorated American gymnast in history. Her example shows how overcoming fears can lead us to more greatness than we can ever imagine.

Reflection for Today: What fear is holding you back from something you dream of doing? Place your thoughts in the notes.

Today's Affirmation: I realize that fear is a natural emotion but will not let it control me. It may knock on my door, but I will not let it in. I understand that courage is not the absence of fear; but pressing on despite it.

NOTES:

<u>YOU ARE INVINCIBLE</u>   <u>~ DAY 10 ~</u>

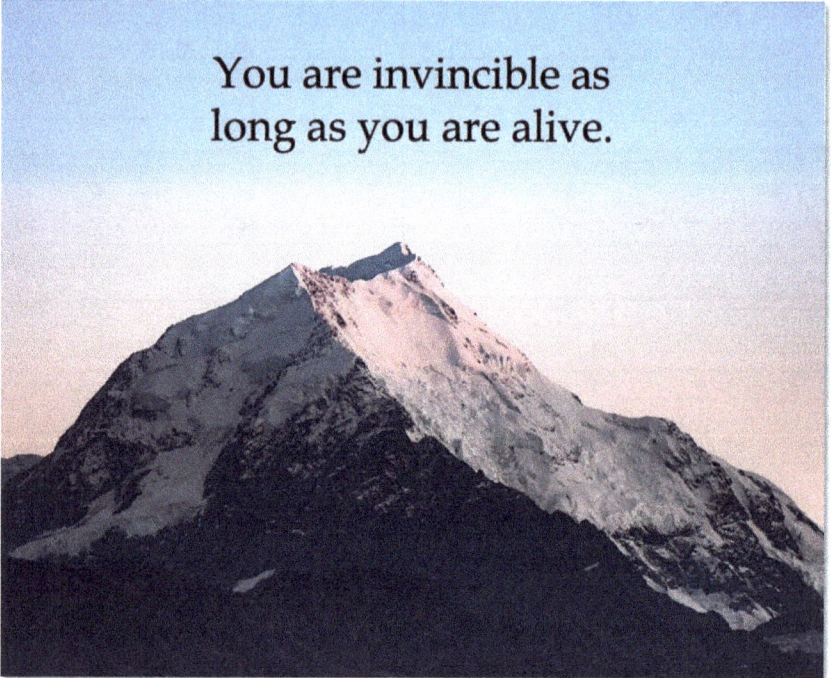

You are invincible as long as you are alive.

You have power over your mind - not outside events.

Realize this, and you will find strength. You are invincible when you master your thoughts.

Marcus Aurelius

Life can often be a roller coaster ride, with unexpected twists and turns that can leave you feeling overwhelmed and powerless. External events can easily dictate your emotions, actions, and overall happiness. But what if you realized that you possess a tremendous power within yourself that can enable you to become invincible?

Your mind is an extraordinary instrument capable of shaping your reality. By acknowledging that you have power over your thoughts, you reclaim control over your life. No matter what happens externally, you can decide how you interpret and respond to it.

This is not a call to ignore reality and blindly accept "feel-good thinking", but to take charge of your internal dialog related to what is happening around you. Instead of succumbing to feelings of defeat, you can view setbacks as valuable lessons that bring wisdom. Instead of constantly replaying dark thoughts in times of distress, you can intentionally change their direction to point to positive outcomes.

The way you perceive the world creates your reality, for good or bad. By consciously choosing positive and empowering points of view, you can become the architect of your own destiny. Ultimately, you are free to make the decision about how you respond to the world and what happens in it.

Limit the number of negative voices you allow into your life. Begin your days with gratitude and hopeful reflection. Remove people or things that create an unhealthy environment. Above all, filter your self-talk to ensure that you are your greatest cheerleader.

Take hold of your thoughts, and you will discover courage that knows no bounds. Uncover your invincibility and achieve more than you can imagine. It is not what happens to you that matters, but how you react to it.

Reflection for Today: What limiting thoughts do you often entertain that keep you from thriving? Write down your answers.

Today's Affirmation: I will hold onto thoughts that build me up. I will not allow negative and critical people or influences to consume my mind. I will live with gratitude and hope to achieve my dreams and goals.

NOTES:

A Better You in 45 Days

BE EXCITED ABOUT YOUR FUTURE ~ DAY 11 ~

Be excited about your future,
not worried about your past.

Be excited about your future, not worried about your past

Every exit is an entry somewhere else.

Tom Stoppard

No one is perfect. Every single person on earth has something in their past that they are not proud of. It can be as simple as a hurtful word spoken, or as life-impacting as a moral failure. The truth is, we are all human and capable of making horrendous blunders.

Ironically, our culture has a habit of demonizing those who fail, while elevating those who overcome failure. But here is the main question: How do you overcome failure if you never fail?

Some of the most popular books and movies in history outline how someone pulled themselves up from adversity to do great things for the world around them. But what is overlooked is that for there to be a victory, there must first be a conflict.

Continuing to relive your indiscretions is like trying to swim while holding a boulder. You will grow weary of fighting the tide and will eventually drown. There is absolutely nothing you can do to alter what has happened in the past. You can only focus on the here and now.

By letting go of what has been, you free yourself to move forward. You can begin to clearly see what lies ahead without a filter of shame and regret. You can also have compassion for others who fail and offer mercy instead of judgement.

In creating a new narrative in your life, you write a hero saga where the one who was broken finds purpose and wins the day. You become the champion of the story and can hold your head up high.

When you take responsibility for your missteps and seek a new direction, not everyone will be glad for you. In fact, you will have many critics arise who will eagerly remind you of how you failed.

Do not let their opinions deter your efforts but remember that they have their own demons to slay. The difference is yours are piled behind you and theirs still hide in the dark.

Reflection for Today: Name the worst mistake you ever made and how you can put it behind you.

Today's Affirmation: I release the grip of the past and let go of regrets, resentments, and what-ifs. I know that dwelling only hinders me. I am deserving of a fresh start and allow myself to heal and create a new life story.

NOTES:

IT'S NOT ABOUT HOW MUCH YOU HAVE~ DAY 12 ~

It's not about how much you have. It's about how much you can give.

Remember that the happiest people are not those getting more, but those giving more.

H. Jackson Brown Jr.

Born on November 25, 1835, in Dunfermline, Scotland, Andrew Carnegie was a prominent American industrialist and philanthropist. He amassed great wealth through his ventures in the steel industry, but he is perhaps best remembered for his remarkable charitable efforts.

Carnegie believed in the concept of "the Gospel of Wealth," which emphasized the responsibility of the wealthy to use their fortunes to benefit society. He exemplified giving back to the community and supported causes that would make a lasting impact on society for generations.

One of Carnegie's most significant acts of generosity was the establishment of over 2,500 libraries worldwide. His aim was to provide free access to knowledge and education for all. These libraries became invaluable resources for communities, fostering literacy and learning.

In addition to libraries, Carnegie donated substantial sums of money to various universities, colleges, and research centers. He also funded the construction of Carnegie Hall in New York City, a renowned concert venue that continues to host world-class performances today. In addition to all of this, he provided grants to aspiring artists, musicians, and writers, enabling them to follow their dreams and contribute to the cultural landscape.

Throughout his life, Carnegie gave away most of his wealth, leaving behind a powerful legacy of generosity. He believed that his fortune should be regarded to improve the well-being of others and advocated for the redistribution of riches for the greater good.

Reflecting on Andrew Carnegie's contributions encourages us to consider the profound impact that our own generosity can have on the world. While we may not have his wealth, we can always offer something of ourselves to enhance the lives of others.

Reflection for Today: What can you do today to become a source of generosity in your circle of influence? List some ways you can start this practice.

Today's Affirmation: I understand that generosity is not limited to material possessions, but encompasses the sharing of my time, knowledge, and compassion. I let go of any attachments to recognition, knowing that the true reward lies in the act of giving and how it impacts the world for good.

NOTES:

A Better You in 45 Days

<u>LOVE YOURSELF</u>   **<u>~ DAY 13 ~</u>**

WHEN YOU LOVE YOURSELF

YOU FIND YOURSELF

When you love yourself, you find yourself.

———— ⌘ ————

And God said love your enemy and I obeyed him and loved myself.

Khalil Gibran

It is crucial to recognize the significance of showing love to yourself. Contrary to what you may have heard, self-love is not selfish; it is an essential component to a fulfilling life. By prioritizing your own well-being and happiness, not only do you enhance your ability to love and care for others, but you also set a powerful example for those around you.

Loving yourself in a healthy way is not arrogance, but a state of deep appreciation for who you are. It involves treating yourself with kindness and respect, just as you would extend to a cherished friend or family member. This affirms your worth and helps you accept your imperfections.

Practicing self-love does not mean you do not take time to care for others. It means that stepping back is important so you can give without being completely drained in the process. Remember, filling your own cup gives you what you need to pour out more compassion and understanding to those who need it.

Caring for yourself is a key component of finding and receiving love. It ensures that you can know true love when it arrives because you have been giving it to yourself all along. You know what behavior you will not tolerate. This will empower you to walk away from anything or anyone that shows themselves to be unloving.

The greatest benefit of properly loving yourself is when someone enters your life to offer you love, you will be able to accept it. You will understand your value and enjoy being seen for how important you are. It will be easier for you to trust and allow that person into your heart. Amazingly, you will also find that it is easier for you to return that love in a genuine way.

The honest care that you afforded yourself will be reflected in all relationships. This allows you the freedom you need to be your authentic self. It all begins with love.

Reflection for Today: What will you do to take care of yourself today? Make a list of practical things you can do.

Today's Affirmation: I am learning how to love myself in the right way and realizing I deserve to be treated with dignity and respect. I am capable of setting and upholding boundaries regarding the type of treatment I will tolerate. I am important.

NOTES:

A Better You in 45 Days

THINK ABOUT ALL THAT YOU ARE ~ DAY 14 ~

Think about all that you are instead of all that you are not.

Think about all that you are instead of all that you are not.

Owning our story and loving ourselves through that process is the bravest thing that we'll ever do.

Brené Brown

How are you doing? I am asking this because, as you travel toward freedom, you should stop every so often to gauge your progress. Here are a few questions to consider:

Do you feel as if your perspective is changing for the good?

Are you more aware of your emotions and thoughts?

Have you begun to eliminate negative or debilitating thought patterns and triggers?

When considering these things, it is vital to keep track of your progress. The important thing is to celebrate that something good is happening to you.

Your daily readings, reflections, and affirmations are meant to guide you, not fix you. You are not broken. Though you may have areas of improvement and consider yourself falling short, you are a work in progress.

In fact, everyone around you is a similar work in progress with their own failings and shortcomings. The difference is you are actively taking steps to expose, confront, and work on yourself.

Sadly, many people do not. This fact alone should make you stand taller and continue to move forward with even more purpose.

Continue the work you began, and you will enjoy the benefits soon enough. Just as a flourishing garden must be weeded, tended, and nourished, so is this new flourishing person you are becoming.

Do not let discouragement or weariness take root in your heart or mind. Each day forward brings you closer to your future and further from your past. I wish you all the best.

~Terry~

Reflection for Today: In what ways can you see yourself becoming more confident and balanced? Write about some of the positive changes you are experiencing.

Today's Affirmation: Every day, I celebrate my progress, no matter how small. I acknowledge the power of self-compassion. I will see discomfort as an opportunity to grow and look forward to the person I am becoming.

NOTES:

THE GIFT OF FORGIVENESS   *~ DAY 15 ~*

Forgiveness is not about anyone else. It is a gift you give yourself.

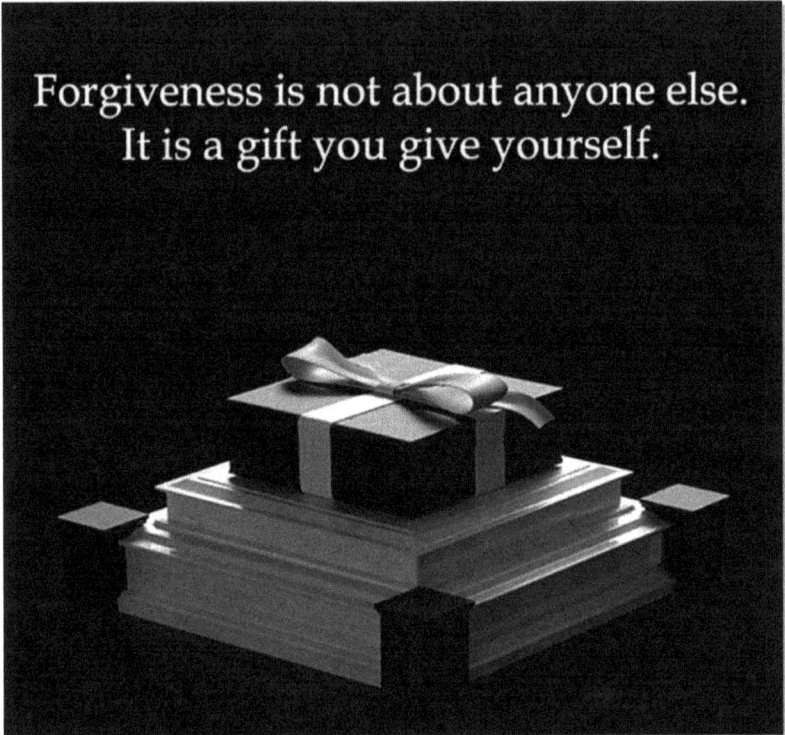

I am who I am today because of the choices I made yesterday.

Eleanor Roosevelt

Do you have something in your life that you wish you could erase? Of course, you do. Everyone does. The problem is not that you made mistakes, but that you may be living under the weight of them. Not forgiving yourself for your past can either suffocate or paralyze you.

Unforgiveness may be a driving force that can drain the joy out of living. This can make you pursue every day with an agenda to prove to yourself that you are perfect. You can become hyper-critical, feeling like there is no room to fail again.

Perhaps you are locked in limbo, afraid to attempt anything new because you believe you are undeserving and inadequate. The ghosts of your past cling to you like shackles and make it impossible to move on.

What makes this worse are the daily reminders of lost opportunities, relationships, or even freedoms that resulted from past choices. This creates a breeding ground for the worst type of unforgiveness: the inability to forgive yourself.

Forgiveness does not mean forgetting or excusing away what happened. You cannot wish away your actions or the harm those actions caused. This means taking responsibility and acknowledging the truth about yourself and what was done.

Dealing with your past is not easy and may entail seeking counseling, support from trusted people, or spiritual guidance to achieve acceptance. This is the first step to silencing the voices that haunt you.

Making these strides will help you begin to live a full life apart from your yesterdays. You will see that you deserve happiness and can achieve greatness. The past version of yourself made decisions based on the circumstances at that time. This new version of you can be something completely different.

Turn your eyes to your future. Your story is still being written. Your entire life is not defined by bad things you have done.

Reflection for Today: What do you need to uncover and forgive yourself for today? Take some time to journal about the experience.

Today's Affirmation: I give myself grace. The person I was in the past lived a different life because decisions were made based on circumstances then. I have matured since those days and will look forward, not backward, any longer.

NOTES:

FORGIVING PEOPLE   ~ DAY 16 ~

Forgiving people who hurt you frees you, not them.

Forgiveness is the fragrance that the violet sheds on the heel that has crushed it.

Mark Twain

Life often bears you down with the weight of past grievances and hurtful events. These emotional burdens can hold you back, preventing you from experiencing the joy you deserve. In these moments, you have a choice: hold onto resentment or offer mercy for those who hurt you.

Forgiving others is not a sign of weakness. When you forgive, you refuse to drink the poison of resentment and bitterness. You release the negativity that consumes your heart and make room for love instead.

Forgiveness does not mean condoning or forgetting the actions that hurt you, but consciously letting go of the debt you feel is owed. By releasing others, you release yourself from the prison of the past. You become an active participant in your own happiness, reclaiming control over your future. This allows you to find inner peace.

Living this way grants you the freedom to seek your own forgiveness for future missteps. You can find grace when you need it because you gave grace to someone else. You will learn to forgive as you are forgiven.

However, this is not a one-time event. It is a lifelong practice that takes time and effort. It requires you to confront what happened, acknowledge it, and gradually release its grip on your heart. This does not mean sticking your head in the sand, but digging up what lies beneath and tackling it once and for all.

What is done is done.

You cannot erase past hurts, but you can take control and move forward despite them. Giving forgiveness to those who caused you harm will set your heart free. Be patient and do not berate yourself for struggling with this. It is not easy.

Forgive even if there is no apology because that is the gift you give to them. Move on without an apology because that is the gift you give to yourself. Your soul deserves peace.

Reflection for Today: What will you do today to forgive someone who has hurt you? Write about the situation and list some ways you can begin to release this burden.

Today's Affirmation:
Forgiveness is a deliberate act that helps my heart heal and sets me free from the past. Letting go of the debt of unforgiveness gives me the power to choose a life filled with compassion, understanding, and love.

NOTES:

A Better You in 45 Days

<u>MAKE LIFE BEAUTIFUL</u>   *~ DAY 17 ~*

Nothing is more beautiful than making life beautiful for others.

The true meaning of life is to plant trees, under whose shade you do not expect to sit.

Nelson Henderson

Terretta Nichelle Howard, aka Terretta Storm, was a powerhouse independent R&B/Rock singer on the cusp of great success in 2019. Along with her boyfriend and manager Kenneth Hawkes, she had just released the video for the most successful single of her career, "Take Me Home". This high-energy anthem showcased her vocal range and captured her vibrant personality like no song before.

Tragically, while crossing a busy street after a late-night performance, Terretta was struck by a car and critically injured. She suffered head trauma, a broken leg, and multiple facial fractures. Paramedics resuscitated her several times on the scene, saving her life.

Sadly, the most horrific result of the accident was that Terretta suffered irreversible brain damage. In her recovery, she had to learn to walk and talk again, but her personality was forever changed. Because of the injuries to her brain, Terretta was no longer the same person, but Kenneth was.

He stayed by Terretta's bedside and prayed openly during the long months she spent in the hospital. He opened his home to care for her once she was released and helped cover her medical expenses. For months afterward, Kenneth worked tirelessly to find a rehabilitation facility for her as well as funding.

Although she may never sing onstage again, Kenneth stays committed to his dear friend. Though he sees the same person on the outside each day, he wrestles with the memory of who she used to be. The fun-loving and vibrant person he had known for so long has been replaced with a stranger. But his unending love and care for Terretta continues to this day.

Kenneth has sacrificed much of his life for Terretta to give her the most beautiful life possible. Despite her adversities and his heart-wrenching pain, he is committed to showing her what love really means.

Reflection for Today: In a similar situation, could you show Kenneth's type of care to someone else? Write about the feelings you experienced while reading this story.

Today's Affirmation: Kenneth and Terretta's story caused me to look outside of myself. I will begin by opening my eyes to the needs of others around me and will do my best to show kindness and love where I can.

Listen to "Take Me Home" by Terretta Storm: https://open.spotify.com/track/6w YqhgueNx5zp1o4zUtepm

NOTES:

A Better You in 45 Days

Denise and Terry Atkins

OUR WOUNDS CAN BE BEAUTIFUL   ~ DAY 18 ~

Our wounds can be the best and most beautiful part of us.

Our scars are a testament to our resilience and the beauty of our healing.

L.R. Knost

pg. 88

The wounds in life, both physical and emotional, can be seen as blemishes or reminders of your darkest times. They can feel like heavy burdens, weighing you down, making it difficult to see a way forward. It is in those moments, however, that you can find ways to heal and grow.

Wounds are not a sign of weakness, but a reminder that you suffered an injury. Instead of being ashamed of them, celebrate them because they also represent a place where healing occurred.

Though your scars may be many, they tell the story of what you endured in your life. You may have felt hopeless while in the middle of the situation, but the scar left behind is a symbol that you made it through.

Embracing your emotional trauma means recognizing the entirety of who you are and what you experienced, good or bad. It means accepting your past, your mistakes, and your imperfections while finding the fortitude to rise above them.

It also means reconciling hurts inflicted on you by others. You may never forget, but you can learn to release it so that your heart can mend. This does not mean minimizing the trauma, but no longer allowing it to consume you. Offering forgiveness is done for you, not them.

Cherishing your wounds allows you to connect with other survivors on a deeper level. When you vulnerably relate your stories, it gives permission for them to do the same. In this act of courage, you become a bridge connecting you to shared experiences and reminding you that you are not alone.

It is often through our darkest moments that we find our brightest light. Your emotional wounds are not burdens to bear, but badges of honor to wear proudly. They do not define you and are not your limitations. Instead, they represent the bravery you found during the battle and the wholeness you carry as your shield today.

Reflection for Today: What is your greatest emotional hurt and how can you help it begin to heal? Explain your answer below.

Today's Affirmation: I will not hide from my life's scars because they are shaping me. I am a masterpiece in progress, and they only enhance my beauty. I am proud of myself and grateful for the heart I have within me.

NOTES:

GROWTH IS A PROCESS   ~ DAY 19 ~

Growth is a process, but it is also progress.

The journey of a thousand miles begins with one step.

Lao Tzu

One of the greatest things about being married to Denise is her love for gardening. Every Spring there is a new light in her eyes as we visit various stores gathering the soil, seeds, and plants needed for that year's garden. I must admit, I also get excited about the prospect of watching the small sprouts break through the soil and grow to maturity as they produce their various vegetables.

For those who are familiar with gardening, there are several steps involved in the planting process. One of the most important is pruning away unnecessary or dead growth to ensure the plants stay healthy. This is an excellent segway for a chapter of our book, so I wanted to include it here.

Dead leaves, unproductive branches, or sick vines steal nutrients from the plant that should be used to make vegetables. If these sections are not cut away, the entire plant could die. Likewise, if too much of the thriving production is removed, the plant could suffer.

Think about your life in this way. Dead or dying relationships or circumstances can steal the energy that should be used for your personal development. If not addressed, you may find yourself exhausted, frustrated, and unable to focus on the things that are important to you.

Removing what is holding you back can be tough. People you must cut off may not respond well or understand your actions. Beginning a new career may set you back financially for a time. Saying no to others may cause friction and test your friendships. But in the end, these are all necessary steps that you must take if you want to flourish.

The pruning of a plant results in the plant looking thin and empty at first, because what appeared to be full has been removed. But in time, as more growth comes in, it becomes apparent that the pruning was necessary. Keep this in mind and begin trimming down your life. What grows afterward is astounding!

~Terry~

Reflection for Today: What pruning can you do in your life's garden today to help you flourish tomorrow? Record some of your thoughts in the notes section.

Today's Affirmation: I am the gardener of my own success. Removing what holds me back is vital to my future. My happiness hinges on my ability to make tough choices and prune away what steals my time and energy. I choose to do what is best for me.

NOTES:

NEW BEGINNINGS   **_~ DAY 20 ~_**

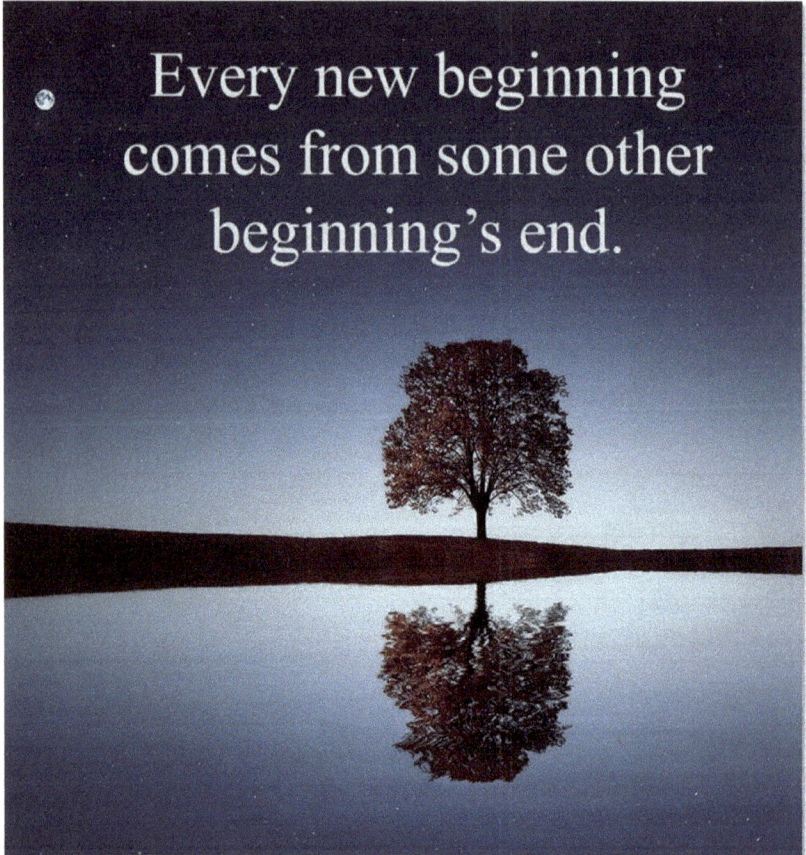

Every new beginning comes from some other beginning's end.

I have not failed. I've just found 10,000 ways that won't work.

Thomas Edison

In the late 1960s, Spencer Silver, a chemist at 3M, was working on developing a strong adhesive. However, his experiments led to the creation of a weak one that did not bond strongly to surfaces. At first glance, this seemed like a failure, and Silver had difficulty finding a practical use for his "low tack" adhesive to no avail.

Years later, another 3M employee named Art Fry attended one of Silver's presentations on the weak adhesive. The crowd listened with varied interest, but Fry was intrigued. He was an avid choir singer and faced a common problem - his bookmarks kept falling out of his hymnal causing him to often lose his place while performing. This inspired Fry to experiment with Silver's creation, and he realized its potential as a removable bookmark.

Fry and Silver collaborated to refine the product and developed small, sticky paper squares that could be easily attached and removed from surfaces without leaving a residue. In 1980, 3M launched their product as "Post-it Notes," and it quickly gained popularity, becoming an iconic office supply item.

Post-it Notes have since become ubiquitous, used by millions of people around the world for reminders, notes, and creative purposes. The accidental discovery of a weak adhesive that was initially seen as a failure turned into a great achievement. It revolutionized the way people organize and communicate.

We can learn from the 3M team's collaboration. Silver's original experiment seemed to end in failure but was the beginning of something world changing. This proves that "failure" does not have to be the end of your dream.

As you seek your heart's desires, you will encounter many hard stops or detours along the way. When they occur, look around to see if another course to victory is in sight. You just might be surprised at what you find.

Reflection for Today: What "failure" in your life can be turned into something useful for the world around you? Describe a plan of action.

Today's Affirmation: I will not be discouraged when things do not go as planned. When opposition comes, I will be open to new possibilities. I will search for creative solutions that can transform disappointment into a remarkable achievement.

NOTES:

OLD WAYS   ~ DAY 21 ~

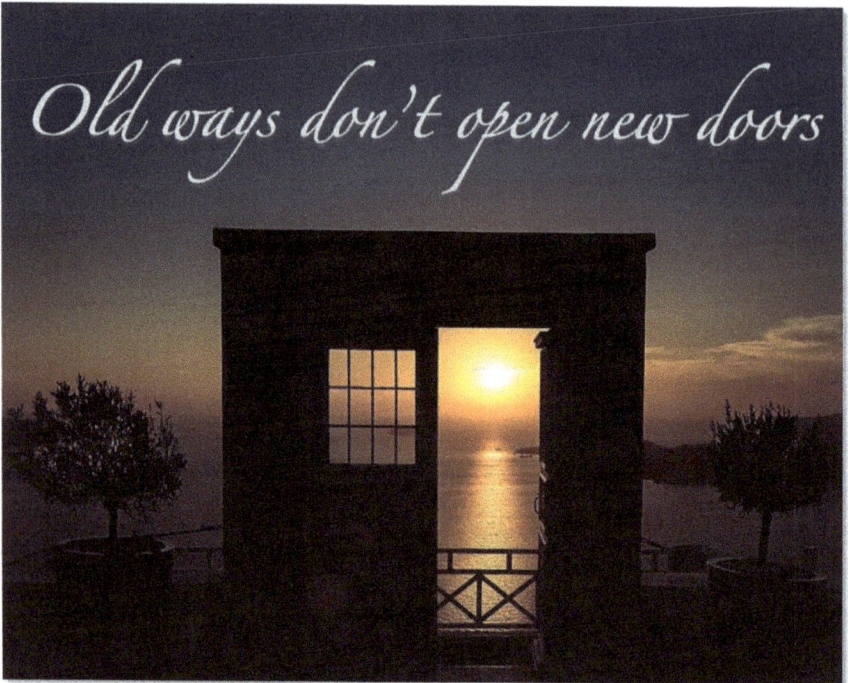

Old ways don't open new doors.

If you do what you have always done, you will get what you have always gotten.

Unknown

Today, we want to share a thought-provoking quote that has resonated with us deeply: "If you do what you have always done, you will get what you have always gotten."

These words, often attributed to Henry Ford and others, serve as a reminder that your actions and choices play a significant role in shaping your outcomes. If you continue to follow the same routines, habits, and patterns, it is inevitable that you will experience the same results. But what if you dare to break free from the familiar and follow the unknown?

Life is ever-changing. Stepping outside of your comfort zones and trying new things will unlock the door to new possibilities. It can be daunting to venture into uncharted territory and let go of what is familiar. However, it is through this willingness to take risks that we can discover who we are and what we are capable of.

Walking into the unknown is an act of courage. Maybe you are thinking about ending a career or relationship. You could be in front of an opportunity to start down an unfamiliar trek. You will never know what life has in store for you if you never take the chance.

Keep in mind that trusting in what is comfortable does not remove the risk of failure. There are plenty of examples of people who never took risks and still had tremendous hardships. Doing nothing is no protection from failure, in fact it may be the greatest failure of all.

We encourage you to reflect upon the quote and consider where it may apply in your own life. Are there areas where you feel stuck or dissatisfied? Are there routines that have become stagnant? Take a moment to envision the possibilities that lie beyond your current actions and repetitive choices.

Remember, it is never too late to reinvent yourself. You are braver than you think. Take chances and watch as new opportunities unfold before your eyes.

Reflection for Today: What routine can you break today to begin expanding your life? Make a list of new activities you can pursue.

Today's Affirmation: I will stop being afraid of new things. I am ready to see what lies ahead for me around the next corner. I understand that "staying safe" can also be stagnation and I will walk through the open doors that life brings my way.

NOTES:

APPRECIATE WHAT YOU HAVE ~ *DAY 22* ~

Appreciate what you have before
life teaches you to appreciate what you lost.

Appreciate what you have before life teaches you to appreciate what you lost.

I'd rather have one tulip right now than a blanket of roses when I'm dead.

Rev. James Cleveland

Think of someone important in your life. What makes them special to you? Why do you cherish them? How would your life be different without them? The main question is: Do they know how you feel?

Expressing your love and gratitude for someone while they are still living is vital. You have probably seen movies or read books where death bed visits from a distant someone include tearful, "would haves", "could haves", or "should haves". The regretful scenes leave the audience grief-stricken but are avoidable with one simple act: Say something before it is too late.

We live in a "throw away" culture that treats relationships like candy wrappers. Many people use what they want and discard the rest. They simply take important people for granted.

Ironically, once those people are removed from their lives, they finally realize what they had. The hole left behind cannot be filled and no amount of wishing can rewind the time lost in their lack of gratitude.

Take a moment to reflect on your own life. Is there someone you take for granted and assume will always be with you? Have you expressed your gratitude to those that matter? Have you thrown away a valuable relationship over something that could easily be resolved? The time to act is now.

Life is short and unpredictable. We live in a "here today, gone tomorrow" culture. You have no idea when that person sitting next to you will no longer be there. When they are gone, the silence will be deafening.

Swallow your pride and let go of grudges. Pick up the phone and call someone you have not talked to in a while. Look into the eyes of the person you care for and say, "I love and appreciate you".

Suffering, illness, divorce, and other losses are inevitable. Show appreciation now to the ones you cherish so that when life happens you will not say, "I should have".

Reflection for Today: Who in your life are you taking for granted? Write down ways that you can begin expressing what they mean to you.

Today's Affirmation: I will express appreciation to those that matter most to me. I will not live in silent gratitude but will use my voice and actions to show how I feel. I understand that time is short and will not live a life of regret.

NOTES:

_____

_____

_____

_____

_____

_____

_____

_____

_____

_____

ALWAYS FIND THE LIGHT ~ DAY 23 ~

> Sunflowers remind us that even on our darkest days, we can find the sunlight.

Sunflowers remind us that even on our darkest days, we can find the sunlight.

Keep your face to the sunshine and you cannot see the shadow. It's what sunflowers do.

Helen Keller

Sunflowers are one of my favorite flowers and have always held a special place in my heart. Their vibrant yellow petals and towering presence never fail to captivate me. The thing that fascinates me most about them is their ability to find sunlight even on the darkest days.

When sunflowers are young, they face East to seek out the morning sun. As the light moves across the sky, their heads turn to follow it. When the flower matures and growth starts to slow down, the older plants continually face East. This is because they react more strongly to light early in the day.

No matter how cloudy, stormy, or gloomy the sky may be, the flower's determination to find the light remains unwavering. Even when night falls, sunflowers remain facing East anticipating the next sunrise.

In life you may have moments of darkness in the form of personal hardships, setbacks, or even tragedies that leave you feeling lost and overwhelmed. During these times, it is easy to succumb to hopelessness and lose your way.

But, just like this flower, you can seek out sunlight, even in your darkest days. It may take effort, but focusing on small rays of light that surround you can gradually illuminate your way forward.

Everyone has dark days, and some are worse than others. Facing the light does not mean ignoring your emotions or pretending to be ok. It means controlling your thoughts and actions while you make your way through the tough times.

Continue to follow the light until you are ready and able to see that you made it out of the dark. Let the sunflower be a reminder that even in the most trying of circumstances, there is always light. You just need to know where to look.

~ Denise ~

Reflection for Today: How can you turn around the darkest tragedies in your life by facing the light as the sunflower does? Record your answers in the notes.

Today's Affirmation: Just like the sunflower, I can defeat any darkness that comes my way. I will set my eyes on the good around me instead of the bad. I can find sunlight even on my darkest days and will continue to shine brightly in every aspect of my life.

NOTES:

A Better You in 45 Days

TAKE THE TIME   *~ DAY 24 ~*

Things worth having take time.

Things worth having, take time.

Patience is not the ability to wait, but the ability to keep a good attitude while waiting.

Joyce Meyer

One of the greatest lessons we can learn is that nature itself does not hurry. Look at the gentle opening of a flower or the growth of a tree. There is a slow and natural pace to the world that is often neglected in our pursuit of immediate results. By observing and aligning ourselves with what nature teaches, we can understand that everything unfolds in its own time.

Patience is not merely the ability to wait but maintaining a sense of calm and composure even when there are delays. It is the understanding that rushing through life only leads to mistakes, stress, and dissatisfaction. Being patient helps us to make wiser decisions, think more clearly, and cherish the journey rather than fixating solely on the destination.

By taking the time to pause, breathe, and be present, we can uncover potential pitfalls prior to acting. When we rush, we may miss a subtle opportunity to learn something new, because we are set on doing things the way we always have.

Also, hurrying through life often leads to burnout and a sense of disconnection. Being busy does not always equal productivity. By intentionally slowing down, we can see and be seen; hear and be heard.

There are things in life that are worth waiting for. For instance, the growth of a fruit tree or the birth of a child. Even finding the right kind of fulfilling relationships could take months or years to develop. But the results of these examples justify the patience invested.

The art of slowing down is a lifelong practice that requires conscious effort and a shift in mindset. Try not to grow weary of the waiting. Enduring to the end helps us find peace in chaos. Life is not a race to be won, but a gift to be treasured. Take a deep breath, slow down, and savor the richness that each moment holds.

Reflection for Today: Write down ways you have shown impatience during the last few days. Also, include your plan on correcting this behavior.

Today's Affirmation: I am grounded, calm, and in tune with the natural rhythm of the world around me. With patience as my guide, I choose to find the blessings and opportunities each day brings. I am patient, I am present, and I am at peace.

NOTES:

A Better You in 45 Days

YOUR KIND OF PAIN   ~ *DAY 25* ~

There are different kinds of pain in this world.
The kind that just hurts and
the kind that changes you.

There are different kinds of pain in this world.
The kind that just hurts and the kind that changes you.

Pain is inevitable. Suffering is optional.

Haruki Murakami

There are different kinds of emotional pain in the world. Such as the kind that lingers and gnaws at your heart or the kind that opens your eyes to see things differently. No one is a stranger to loss, tragedies, or failure. Unfortunately, this is life.

Whatever you endure, surviving trauma or disappointment can alter you in a good or bad way. This is ultimately up to you to choose. You can use the hurt you experienced to help others survive their hardships, or you can let it become your greatest weapon as you build walls and stop caring for anyone but yourself.

When you are just hurting it is easy to feel consumed by despair and hopelessness. You can retreat into the shadows and shield yourself to avoid further suffering. This type of response can lead you to selfish and destructive acts where your needs are the priority regardless of how they affect others.

On the other hand, your trauma can be fuel for transformation. Anguish can refine you into becoming stronger and open your eyes to what others are going through. Every tear you shed, and every heartache you endured, has the capacity to increase love and empathy. But you must be open to it.

When troubles come, it is crucial to remember that you are not alone. By extending compassion and understanding for the plight of another, you give meaning and purpose to your own adversity. What you endured becomes valuable and allows your life to be a lighthouse in someone else's storm.

What is meant to destroy you can push you to do greater things. Instead of looking at your trials as negatives, reflect on what you learned from them. By changing your perspective, you can turn your pain into passion and your heartache into the light it needs to be. In this way you can inspire others to do the same.

Reflection for Today: How can you use what you have been through to help someone else today? Give a specific example and actions you can take.

Today's Affirmation: I will view the scars of my past as badges of honor. Each one contributes to the unique story of my life. Without them I would not have learned my own strength.

NOTES:

A Better You in 45 Days

THE RIGHT KIND OF NO ~ DAY 26 ~

Sometimes the right kind of no
is better than the wrong kind of yes.

Sometimes the right kind of no is better than the wrong kind of yes.

When you say yes to others, make sure you are not saying no to yourself.

Paulo Coelho

Saying no can be difficult. It often creates friction and discomfort. Not learning this word can leave you exhausted as you frequently overcommit your energy, time, and resources. But there is hope. You have the power to break the cycle of pleasing others.

Saying no is not a sign of weakness or selfishness. It honors your own limits and ensures you have what is needed to invest in yourself.

Here are some practical ways you can begin to unleash your "No":

Start Small: Begin by saying no to smaller requests or commitments. This allows you to build confidence and enjoy the peace that comes with setting boundaries.

Use Assertive Communication: When declining an offer, be clear, direct, and respectful. Practice saying no in a calm and confident tone, maintaining eye contact and open body language.

Offer Alternatives or Compromises: If you feel comfortable, suggest options that may still meet the needs of others while respecting your own boundaries. This shows that the relationship is valuable, and you are willing to find a mutually beneficial solution.

Be Prepared for the Fallout: A person's reaction to your "no" will expose their motives and expectations. If someone reacts badly to your refusal, then you probably made the best choice. You are not required to say "yes" just to appease someone else.

Learn from Experience: Reflect on the times you said no. Remember the positive outcomes. Use these lessons to continue setting boundaries and protecting your personal time.

Give yourself permission to set healthy boundaries in all areas of your life – personal, professional, and everything in between. Time is a precious commodity, and you deserve to devote it to things and people that you deem important.

Reflection for Today: Is there something or someone you should say "no" to today? Journal your thoughts in the notes section.

Today's Affirmation: I honor my boundaries and prioritize my well-being. Saying no is important. Each time I say no, I create space for activities and relationships that bring me genuine joy and fulfillment.

NOTES:

A Better You in 45 Days

LIFE DOES NOT HAVE TO END   ~ DAY 27 ~

Your life does not have to end because someone is no longer in it.

Your life does not have to end because someone is no longer in it.

Healing doesn't mean the damage never existed.
It means the damage no longer controls our lives.
Akshay Dubey

One of life's toughest challenges is moving on after losing someone dear - whether it is due to death, break up, or estrangement. It is not an easy road to navigate but know that you are not alone. Everyone will go through grief.

The first thing to remember is that sadness and loneliness are natural responses to any loss. It is important to give yourself permission to experience them fully. Cry, shout, or do whatever helps you release those emotions in a healthy way. Above all, allow yourself time to grieve as you need to.

Next, hold on to the beautiful or special memories. Do not let them fade away. Use them as a reminder of the love and joy you shared. That loved one was a part of your story, and they will always have a special place in your heart.

While it may be easy to blame or feel guilty, it is crucial to be kind to yourself with gentleness and understanding. Find joy in the little things. Be sure to take care of your well-being by continuing to engage in activities you enjoy.

Remember, you do not have to go through this alone. Seek support from your loved ones, friends, or even therapy groups. Surround yourself with people who have been there. Find others who can lift you up, listen to you, and offer a shoulder to lean on. Sharing your feelings and stories can make a world of difference.

Everyone grieves in their own way. There is no timeline or instruction manual. Whatever you do, try to continue moving forward. Reconnect with who you are as an individual and create a new narrative for your life.

Lastly, don't shy away from the change. Life will never be the same, and that is ok. Some are meant to be in your life for a short time, while others are meant to be there for a lifetime. You are stronger than you know, and moving through grief can shape you into an even more incredible person.

Reflection for Today: Write the name of a loved one you lost and allow any emotions to flow freely. Record some of the memories that come to mind.

Today's Affirmation: I can move forward after parting ways with a loved one. I will not put a time limit on my grief, but I will also not allow it to consume me. I will work through the loss and cherish the memories we shared.

NOTES:

THE STRENGTH YOU NEED   ~ DAY 28 ~

You never know your true strength until you need it.

You never know how strong you are until being strong is your only choice.

Bob Marley

You may not realize how strong you are until you find yourself in a situation that demands strength. When life is good, it is easy to go about your daily routines without a care. But the depth of your courage can only be discovered in tough times.

There's a certain beauty in not knowing how strong you are until you must be. It is like a dormant force waiting patiently, biding its time until called upon. It's when the moment arrives and life throws its toughest blows your way, that you are forced to stand and fight.

Fearlessness may start with a glimmer of hope that emerges from the depths of uncertainty, or a fiery resolve that flares in the middle of a conflict. But in trying moments, you realize that there is something within you that pushes back refusing to crumble.

Toughness reveals itself in different forms. It can be the choice to keep going, even when every fiber of your being begs you to give up. Or it can be the quiet courage to confront your fears head-on, despite the trembling in your heart.

It may be difficult to comprehend the extent of your own limits until you witness them in action. You surprise yourself with the tenacity you possess that allows you to bounce back from the most devastating blows. This is a reminder that you are capable of more than you can ever imagine.

But perhaps the most remarkable aspect of discovering your bravery is the transformative energy it holds. You no longer see yourself as a powerless victim of circumstance. Instead, you become a warrior, ready to conquer whatever life throws your way with a roar.

If you ever doubt your own strength again, remember that it is lying within you waiting for the perfect moment to emerge. Trust in yourself and know that you have what it takes to win in this life.

Reflection for Today:
Describe a time recently when you leaned on toughness you did not know you had.

Today's Affirmation: I will be courageous and trust in myself and my abilities. I have overcome many things in my past and will do so again. I am a fighter and can win in life.

NOTES:

<u>SOMETIMES THERE ARE NO WORDS</u>   *~ DAY 29 ~*

Sometimes there are no words to describe your feelings.

Sometimes there are no words to describe your feelings.

The silence between the notes is as important as the notes themselves.

Wolfgang Amadeus Mozart

As you continue to work through this journal, you may find yourself failing to find ways to express your feelings at times. Silence can be intimidating. However, by accepting it as a valid form of communication, you begin to accept the idea that sometimes silence speaks louder than words.

Imagine sitting by a serene lake, watching the ripples of water, and feeling a sense of tranquility wash over you. In that moment, you do not need to explain or describe your feelings– you can simply be present and allow calm to envelop you and give you peace.

Silence provides an opportunity to enjoy mindfulness. This allows you to observe your thoughts and emotions without judgment. In quiet times you can gain a deeper understanding of your heart, mind, and life in general. It may feel uncomfortable at first, but removing the noise of the world around you is a valuable and beneficial practice.

Creative expression can become another powerful outlet for peace. Whether through art, music, or movement, engaging in creative activities can allow you to channel your emotions. These practices can also help you unlock your feelings when words fail you.

Set aside a few minutes each day for mindfulness meditation. Sit in a quiet space, close your eyes, and focus on your breath. Allow any thoughts and feelings to arise. Instead of engaging with them, simply acknowledge them and continue to keep your mind at rest. This practical exercise can help you become more comfortable with your inner silence.

Life is often filled with the noise and chaos of this world. Your mind can become burdened with the constant cares of everyday living. Cherish the quiet moments because they can have the greatest impact on your piece of mind. Sometimes silence really is golden.

Reflection for Today: When can you set aside 15 to 30 minutes today for silent meditation and reflection? Write about some of the areas in your life that are causing the most stress.

Today's Affirmation: I will not be afraid of silence. I trust the power of quiet moments to guide me towards inner peace and understanding. In the silence, I find my voice even when words elude me.

NOTES:

A Better You in 45 Days

<u>***YES YOU CAN***</u>   *~ DAY 30 ~*

When someone says you "can't", tell them that word is not in your vocabulary.

When someone says you "can't", tell them that word is not in your vocabulary.

The mind is everything. What you think, you become.

Buddha

In the 2015-2016 English Premier League football season, Leicester City shocked the world by winning the title against all expectations.

At the start of the season, Leicester City was considered a relegation candidate, meaning they were expected to fail and potentially drop down to a lower league. The team narrowly avoided relegation the previous season, and many experts predicted that they would face a similar fate.

However, the Leicester City players, led by their manager Claudio Ranieri, approached the season with a strong belief in their abilities. They remained focused on their strengths and set their collective sights on achieving the seemingly impossible.

Throughout the year, Leicester City exhibited a remarkable display of teamwork and sheer determination. They were proud of the underdog status and used it as motivation to prove the doubters wrong.

As the season progressed, Leicester City continued to defy expectations. Again and again, they defeated some of the league's top teams. Each victory fueled their confidence and gave them the drive to keep believing.

Despite injuries to key players, the team never lost faith. Their positive mindset was contagious and spread throughout the entire soccer club, from the players to the coaching staff and even the fans.

In the final stages of the season, Leicester City's consistent performances placed them at the top of the league table. On May 2, 2016, they secured the Premier League title with two games to spare, completing one of the most remarkable achievements in European football history.

Leicester City's triumph was a testament to the power of positivity and belief. Their story reminds us that almost anything is possible once we decide not to give up. Our success will silence those who don't believe, and our story has the power to inspire generations.

Reflection for Today: What is a limiting belief that has kept you from pursuing a dream? Describe it below.

Today's Affirmation: Like Leicester City, I will stay focused and stand knowing that I can achieve the extraordinary. I will use their story as a reminder that I have the talent and drive to create my own success.

NOTES:

RECOGNIZE YOUR WORTH   *~ DAY 31 ~*

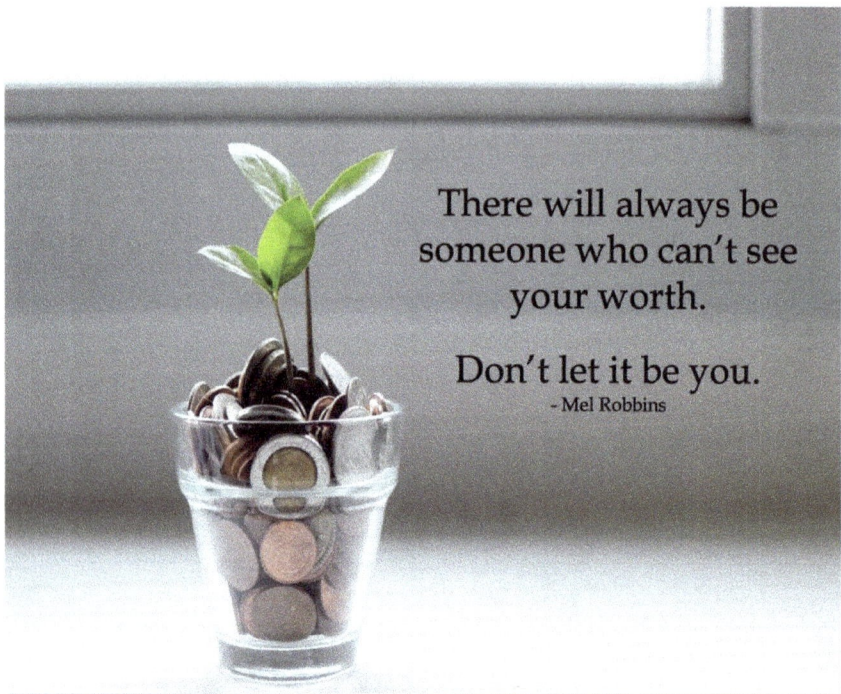

There will always be someone who can't see your worth. Don't let it be you.

Never allow someone else's limited perception to define your worth.

Virginia Satir

Others not seeing your worth can be a disheartening experience. It can make you feel overlooked, as if your contributions and abilities go unnoticed. Nothing is more frustrating than putting in your best efforts and not receiving the recognition you feel you deserve.

One possible reason for being underappreciated is people may have their own preconceived notions that prevent them from seeing your value. They may have certain expectations or stereotypes about what "worth" looks like. If you do not fit into those molds, they may diminish you.

Sometimes others are simply too caught up in their own concerns and priorities to notice your importance. They may not be intentionally ignoring your contributions but are unable to be aware of them.

It is possible that others do not see your impact because you have not effectively communicated it to them. This can involve speaking up about your achievements or highlighting your skills. Not to be confused with boasting, actively promoting your abilities can increase the chances of others recognizing your input.

Understand that you deserve love and respect but be careful not to seek validation from others in an unhealthy way. This can cause you to rely on external sources to define you. Embrace the idea that you are enough, just as you are. Remember this when moments of doubt or disappointment creep in.

Surround yourself with positive influences and supportive people who uplift and encourage you. Seek out individuals who benefit from, and express their thanks for, the impact you have on their lives.

Believe in yourself and know that even your smallest contributions matter. See your worth regardless of the opinions of others. It is not theirs to determine. You are more than you know.

Reflection for Today: How can you ignore the cynics and recognize your worth? List ways you can bring your contributions to the minds of others.

Today's Affirmation: I acknowledge my unique qualities and what they bring to the world. I am enough, just as I am. I deserve the good things life has to offer and treasure them as they come my way.

NOTES:

GATHER THE STONES   ~ *DAY 32* ~

Let the stones they threw at you become the stepping stones to your success.

Let the stones they threw at you become the stepping stones to your success.

Let people underestimate you.
That way they'll never know for sure what you're capable of.
Naiyer Asif

The confetti fell as the Kansas City Chiefs celebrated a 25-22 win over the San Francisco 49ers at the end of Superbowl LVII. Cameras flashed and reporters crowded in on the stars of the winning team hoping to get perfect photos and soundbites. But, amid the celebration, the greatest success story was somehow being overlooked.

Brock Purdy, the 24-year-old quarterback for the Niners, played college football for the Iowa State Cyclones. He was selected as the final pick in the 2022 NFL draft, (262nd overall). Players picked in this position are called, "Mr. Irrelevant", often being released before pre-season or training camps even begin. But injuries to the first- and second-string quarterbacks pushed Purdy into the starting lineup and opened the door for a Cinderella Story.

Scouting reports from other teams stated that Brock was not a very good athlete and had a limited arm, both in strength and throw repertoire. The critics admitted that Purdy had decent speed for college but expected the NFL defenses to be too much for him. But the more he played, the more the scouts were proven very wrong.

Purdy became the first 'Mr. Irrelevant' to throw a touchdown pass in a regular season game. He was also the only first career quarterback to beat a team led by Tom Brady when the 49ers defeated the Tampa Bay Buccaneers 35–7. Purdy became the second player in NFL history, after Aaron Rodgers, to record a cumulative total quarterback rating of 115 or greater in his first two starts.

In the 2022-2023 season, Brock Purdy took his team to the NFC Championship. In 2024, he became the lowest drafted quarterback to ever start a Super Bowl. Against a tough and veteran defense, Purdy completed 23-of-38 passes for 255 yards and one touchdown in the overtime loss to Kansas City. Though the media focused on the back-to-back wins of the Chiefs, the extraordinary rise of this unassuming field general was the greater accomplishment. He was an MVP in his own right.

The playing statistics of this 24-year-old quarterback are astounding, but he remains grounded in his faith and filled with humility. "Life is about being a part of something bigger than yourself.", Purdy said after the Superbowl. "You get wrapped up in getting all the glory and the fame and status. I feel like that's a shallow life and that can fade away pretty quickly."

Purdy's coaches admit they underestimated his agility and mental toughness, but when opportunity knocked, Brock Purdy showed the NFL, and the world, that he was extremely relevant.

Reflection for Today: How do others underestimate your abilities and talents? Write about a time you were able to prove the doubters wrong.

Today's Affirmation: Like Brock Purdy, I will push past the critics and grab hold of success. I will also remain humble, remembering that no matter how high I rise, I can always fall. Those that underestimate me do not know what I am capable of, and their low opinions do not define me.

NOTES:

_____

_____

_____

_____

_____

_____

_____

_____

_____

_____

_____

_____

_____

_____

_____

_____

_____

_____

_____

KNOW THE TRUTH   ~ DAY 33 ~

Know the truth about yourself so you can better recognize the lies.

Know the truth about yourself so you can better recognize the lies.

Knowing yourself is the beginning of all wisdom.

Aristotle

Today's writing will be longer than usual. It outlines how harmful and careless words can cause long term emotional damage. If you are not careful, this trauma can be carried with you throughout your life.

Have you ever been told the same negative things so often that you start to believe them? You hear hurtful voices telling you so many lies that you have a hard time hearing yourself telling the truth.

Growing up, I recall a few distant family members who often made degrading and demeaning comments about me. Though I was brought up in a loving family, the hurtful remarks made me believe I was not pretty, smart, or good enough for anyone to love me. Their lies began to feel true which shaped a twisted perception of myself and the world around me.

At first, I did not question these falsehoods which became a part of my reality, coloring every aspect of my life. As a child I believed I was unworthy of love, success, or happiness. I internalized the negativity, and let it grow until it became a self-fulfilling prophecy. I held myself back, afraid to take risks or pursue my dreams because I believed I would inevitably fail.

Sadly, the untruths that were imprinted in my mind as a child bled into my adult life. Many relationships I made were built around the worthless perception I had of myself. I became an unrecognizable person filled with many regrets. I allowed others to make me feel small and the confidence I once knew as a fun-loving little girl was buried deep inside me.

Finally, as I grew older, I began to realize that the lies were just that - lies. They were the product of other people's insecurities and limiting beliefs. With courage, I began to challenge the validity of the damaging messages that were drummed into my head for so long.

It was not an easy process. I had to suffer many losses and endure life-changing heartbreaks to realize how valuable I was. I went to therapy to help unravel the tangled web of deception that wrapped my soul. With the help of my faith in God, and the continual words of encouragement from my loving husband, Terry, I began building a new wall of truth around my heart and mind.

It was difficult at first. I had to confront deep-rooted beliefs and face them head-on. I also surrounded myself with positive people who believed in me and encouraged me to see my own value. Slowly I began to dismantle the limiting cage that held me captive for so long.

I replaced the words of inadequacy with affirmations of inspiration and empowerment. I created a healthy environment and removed people from my life that constantly spoke trouble into my heart. Over time, the hurtful and degrading voices began to lose their power.

I realized that I could achieve great things. I finally saw that I deserved happiness and success just like everyone else. The falsehoods that once felt so true now seemed absurd. They were like a distant echo from a past I was determined to leave behind.

Today, I still carry the scars of inadequacy and doubt, but they no longer define me. I learned to expose and confront the scoffers whenever they attempt to resurface. I know that my worth is not determined by the opinions of others or the false narratives that they try to impose upon me.

I share this personal experience with you not to receive sympathy, but to empower you. Regardless of your past, stop listening to the accusations of others concerning who you are. Learn the truth about yourself and commit to growing into the best version of you.

My process of overcoming the damage of lifelong lies has taught me the importance of self-love. It has shown me that I have the power to rise above the noise of doubters. I am no longer defined by the lies that once felt true, but by the strength I discovered within myself to rewrite my own story. Now it is your turn.

~ Denise ~

Reflection for Today: What lies do you need to reject to see the truth about yourself? Create a list of your positive attributes and accomplishments.

Today's Affirmation: I will be consciously aware of the untruths that may cloud my perception of myself. I reject these falsehoods and speak the truth about who I am. I release any doubt or limiting beliefs that hold me back because I am enough.

NOTES:

ENJOY THE RIDE   ~ DAY 34 ~

Life is like a roller coaster full of ups and downs.
You can scream or enjoy the ride.

Life is not about waiting for the storm to pass;
it's about learning to dance in the rain.
Vivian Greene

We have a small sign in our living room that says. "Our family must be God's favorite sitcom", and there are days when I agree. Just like any good sitcom, there are moments of sadness followed by riotous laughter that keeps the audience guessing. Those light-hearted times are what help keep the darker times in balance.

I love to laugh, and being with Denise is the most fun I have ever had with another human being. We joke, sing, and dance every day as our dogs watch us with utter curiosity. That is our life together. We are determined to live, love, and laugh until we cannot any longer.

What is amazing is that both of us have endured tremendous pain and heartbreak. From death of family members to divorce and estrangement, there are plenty of things in our lives that could steal our laughter. Thankfully, we are both wired to laugh first and cry later which helps us lean on one another during the downs of life.

For instance, there have been times when I had to make seemingly impossible choices regarding distancing myself from some of my family. Denise held me close and loved me through the hurt. She listened intently, held my hand, and guided me along. Then, she launched into one of her infamous alter egos and had me crying tears of laughter instead of sorrow. The laughing helped get me through the difficulties and I am glad to say I have done the same for her on many occasions. We always hold each other up.

I admit, what we have together is very special and unique, but I believe it is something everyone can find and enjoy. Be advised, the key to this kind of happiness is vulnerability and that can be terrifying.

If you are longing for genuine happiness, it is going to require you to be open and honest with yourself during the good days and the bad. You will also need people in your life that you can be real with. These people need to know how to listen to you and speak the truth when you need it.

Everyone is riding life's rollercoaster. When the ups and downs come, do not let the downs consume you, but enjoy what the ups can bring. Learn to be vulnerable and trust your feelings to those who truly love you.

Just like in an amusement park, the rides are more fun with a friend. Choose those who choose you and make a space for them to come along. Going through the bad times can lead to good times, especially when you are with someone special.

~Terry~

Reflection for Today: Think of a recent "down" where someone helped you turn it into an "up" and write it below.

Today's Affirmation: I believe that a full life has its share of good and bad experiences. I will open myself and my feelings to trusted people who love and value me. Then we can enjoy this ride of life together.

NOTES:

KEEP YOURSELF SAFE   ~ DAY 35 ~

In order to heal you must stay away from the people or things that broke you.

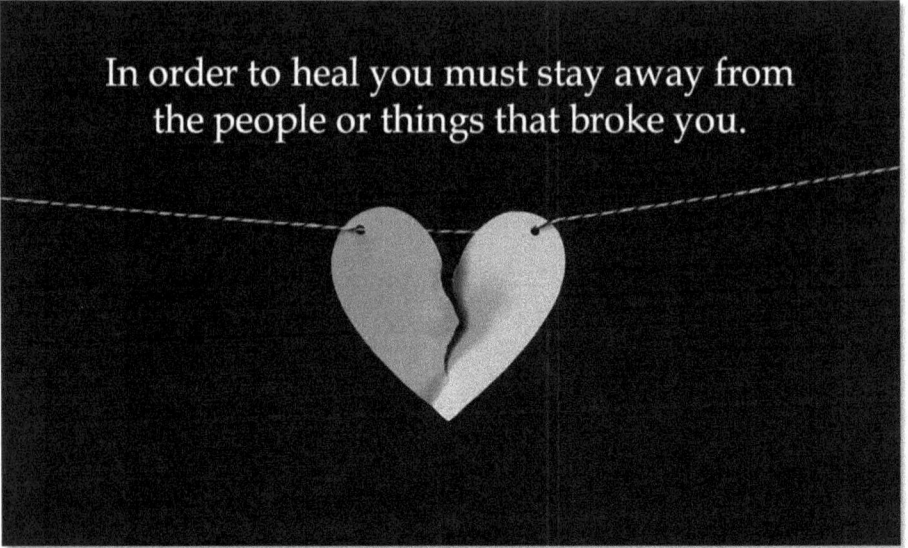

Healing is a journey, and sometimes that journey requires leaving behind the people and things that hinder your progress.
Mandy Hale

There are various individuals and experiences you encounter that shape you. Some bring immense love and support, while others may cause turmoil, or heartache. It is in these moments of hurt that you must find the courage to prioritize your well-being above all else.

Just as a physical wound requires time to heal, your emotional wounds also need space and time to mend. It is essential to acknowledge that healing is a process unique to everyone. There are times this will require you to distance yourself from people or things that continue to poison your heart and soul.

This does not mean you are weak or running away. On the contrary, it takes courage to admit that certain relationships or situations are harmful. By creating personal boundaries, you protect your own mental and emotional health.

Everyone deserves to be in a caring environment that allows you to flourish. Creating boundaries and saying no to what harms you are important steps toward building a safe space.

When removing harmful people or circumstances from your life, there may be moments of doubt, loneliness, and longing. During these times, it is crucial to lean on trusted people who build you up and will tell you the hard truths without platitudes. Connect with individuals who share your values and genuinely love you without judgement.

Your wellness should take priority. It is less important to worry about the feelings of others when their presence in your life causes you strife. These decisions to separate are not always easy but are sometimes necessary.

As you distance yourself from what has hurt you, you will be redefined. Healing takes time and is not simply a destination. Once you remove negative influences from your life, you will see that the short-term decision will be worth a lifetime of peace.

Reflection for Today: To have a more productive life, who or what can you distance yourself from? Explain how your life will be better once you have done this.

Today's Affirmation: Though it may be difficult at first, I will do my best to surround myself with positive and supportive individuals. I will set clear boundaries and say no to harmful people or situations. I will keep myself safe.

NOTES:

<u>*JUST 1% BETTER*</u>   <u>*~ DAY 36 ~*</u>

> Don't try to
> be perfect.
> Just try to be
> 1% better
> each day.

Don't try to be perfect. Just try to be 1% better each day.

Every day, in every way, I'm getting better and better.

Emile Coue

When you begin the process of improving yourself, it is easy to get bogged down by what you have to "fix" in your life. You realize that there are many flaws in your personality and mindset that must be confronted. This understanding of your own frailty can be disheartening at least, and overwhelming at most.

Keep in mind, the goal is not perfection but simply improvement. Perfection is an illusion and an unattainable standard. No one on the entire face of this planet is perfect. So, instead of focusing on how far you must go, pay attention to how far you have come. Look back to the first few pages of this journal and see what you wrote down. Compare that to what you are writing now. Has at least one thing gotten better for you? If so, then you have improved.

The most important thing to keep in mind is that you are not competing against anyone, even yourself. You are not being scored or graded. No one is going to challenge your feelings or try to sway your opinions. You are simply taking some time to add reflective exercises to your day that could help your quality of life. Nothing more.

Keep up the good work through the good days and the tough days. There will always be moments when you stumble, encounter obstacles, or feel discouraged. During these times you will get to see your progress in action.

Maybe a conflict arose, you took a deep breath and did not react like you usually do. Perhaps you thought about yourself in a more positive way or gave someone a little more grace than usual. All these things can be considered progress in the right direction. Do not discount them. Each small step brings you closer to where you want to be.

You are doing the work and seeing the rewards. You did not come this far to only come this far. Stay the course and be encouraged.

Reflection for Today: In what areas have you improved most since beginning this book? Write them down.

Today's Affirmation: I will continue to focus on the process of changing and notice how far I have come. I will remember that no one is perfect, and I will strive to be better today than I was yesterday.

NOTES:

A Better You in 45 Days

THE FIRST THING   ~ DAY 37 ~

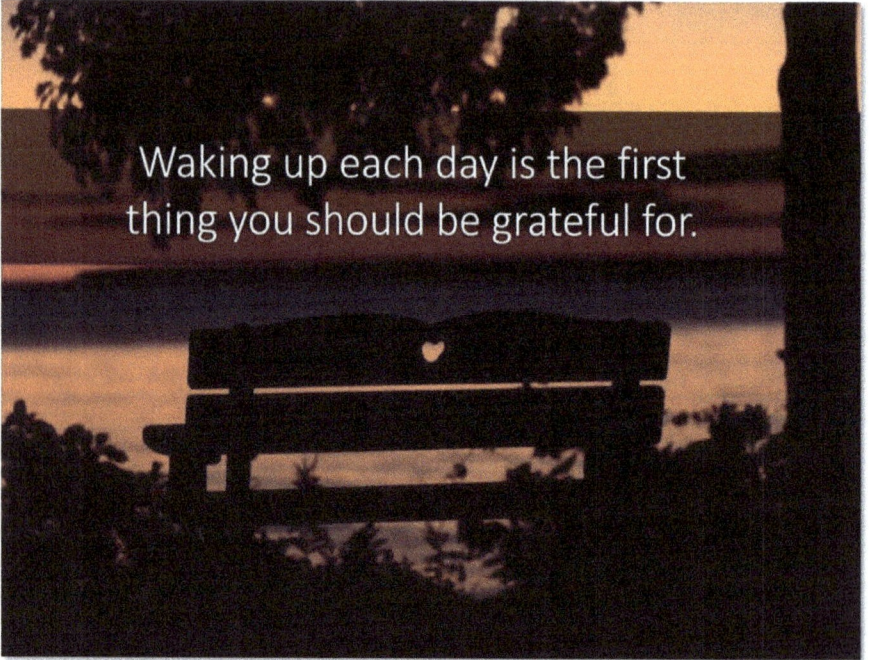

Waking up each day is the first thing you should be thankful for.

Every morning, you have two choices:

continue to sleep with your dreams or wake up and chase them.

Arnold Schwarzenegger

The most amazing thing happened to you today. YOU WOKE UP!

Whether you are an early riser or a "one more snooze" type of person, the wonderful thing is you have an entire day in front of you that is about to unfold. Yesterday is forever gone. Tomorrow is not promised, and so all you truly have is right now, today.

What will you do with it? Do you have big plans, or will you complete some small tasks on your To Do List? Are you making major moves in your life, or are you taking it easy to let yourself rest and reflect?

No matter what today looks like for you, the great news is you are here to experience it. That is the power of living. You are in control of your thoughts and actions regardless of what the day brings.

Here are a few things you can do to begin each day in a positive and productive light:

Before getting busy, write down 3 things you are grateful for. They can be big or small - your health, a roof over your head, your friends and family, even a cup of coffee. Expressing gratitude shifts your mindset.

Say affirming words in the mirror to yourself like "Today is a good day. I am excited for the opportunities this day will bring." Having a positive outlook attracts positive experiences.

Move your body. Go for a walk or do some stretches. Getting your blood flowing in the morning can boost your energy and mood for the whole day.

Practice deep breathing. Taking a few mindful breaths for several minutes can calm you and prepare you to meet what may unfold.

You have been gifted with another day. Begin with appreciating the fact that it is yours to enjoy. Remember, one good day after another creates an incredible life in the end.

Reflection for Today: Write down three things you are grateful for today and take a moment to reflect on them.

Today's Affirmation: I begin this new day with a grateful heart. I treasure the simple gift of being alive. I will slow down and notice the beauty around me. I am thankful for this chance to see another sunrise.

NOTES:

LOOKING FORWARD   ~ DAY 38 ~

Let go of what was.
Be grateful for what is.
Look forward to what is next.

Let go of what was. Be grateful for what is.
Look forward to what is next.

Gratitude makes sense of our past, brings peace for today,

and creates a vision for tomorrow.

Melody Beattie

Let it go. This is harder than it sounds. Everyone has a past, and we often find ourselves holding onto it. Whether our past was hurtful or happy, we can get caught up in the what-ifs or nostalgia and forget to witness the beauty right in front of us.

First, letting go does not mean forgetting or dismissing the importance of what was. It means acknowledging that the past has shaped us and taught us valuable lessons. Releasing the grip on what was frees us from regret and sorrow. When we let go, we create space for something new to come our way.

Next, being grateful means not only releasing the past, but fully embracing the present. When you begin to relish the little things in life, they become bigger than the old problems that still haunt us. Suddenly, the trivial worries that once consumed us begin to fade and are replaced by a deep appreciation for the now.

Gratitude is not arrogance or haughtiness but is the acknowledgement of what we have rather than what we lack. When we are thankful, we become aware of the things we often take for granted. Life is not only about counting our blessings, though. It is also about expressing thanks to those who made a difference along the way.

Looking forward is not simply goal setting. It is focusing on the present while eagerly awaiting the possibilities of tomorrow. Living in anticipation of good things is an essential practice for a fulfilling and meaningful life. This keeps hope alive in our hearts.

Lastly, try to view life as a series of chapters in a book. Some are filled with darkness and peril while others have joy and victory. Accept the uncertainty of tomorrow and trust that what lies ahead is more beautiful than what has been left behind. The entire story is what matters most.

Yours is still being written.

Reflection for Today: Which do you need to work on most; Letting go of the past, being grateful for today, or looking forward to your future? Describe your answer below.

Today's Affirmation: I am letting go of the past, gratefully embracing the present, and eagerly welcoming what the future holds. I release the burdens that no longer serve me, and I am open to the beauty and joy that each moment brings.

NOTES:

A Better You in 45 Days

JUST BE YOU   ~ DAY 39 ~

Instead of conforming to please others, just be you.

Instead of conforming to please others, just be you.

Be yourself: everyone else is already taken.

Oscar Wilde

Choosing self-improvement is a noble endeavor. It represents that you looked inward and recognized things about yourself that you were not satisfied with. This caused you to begin the work of changing. You should be proud of these first steps, but also be prepared. Not everyone is going to cheer you on.

In fact, you will probably be amazed at the number of people who look at you strangely and ask, "Why do you need to be different? You are fine just the way you are." As an agent of change, you are in a minority. Most people will never be honest enough with themselves to put effort into being different.

You probably know people who complain about their weight, but never choose to diet and exercise. Others express dissatisfaction with their careers or relationships but will stay for years just because it is easy. They are comfortably unhappy and will do nothing to break out of the rut.

It is also a sad truth, but people will often try to pull someone else down instead of lifting themselves up. This can be due to jealousy or laziness; lack of confidence or self-worth; or simply the fear of the unknown. Regardless of their motives or actions, you must be steadfast in your commitment to the process of improvement. Something sparked inside of you that drove you to action, so do not lose that fire.

Furthermore, beware of your own discouraging thoughts. Your inner voices can often grow dark as time moves on. Your tough days will hinder you most. Those will be the moments that you are tempted to throw in the towel and give up. Don't do it.

There will be many oppositions that can make your progression forward very difficult. Press ahead through the doubts because where you are going is greater than where you have been.

You have come too far to turn back now.

Reflection for Today:
Describe how you can overcome the temptation to conform or revert to old ways to please others.

Today's Affirmation: I am proud of the work I have done so far. I recognize the ways that I am different than I was before. I will use these changes as inspiration when doubts and doubters try to creep in.

NOTES:

A Better You in 45 Days

A LIFE THAT YOU LOVE ~ DAY 40 ~

Create a life you don't need to escape from.

The biggest adventure you can ever take is to live the life of your dreams.

Oprah Winfrey

When you think of a good life, what do you imagine? Is it having extra money in the bank or being able to travel the world in leisure? Maybe your version of a perfect existence includes a loving spouse or children you can be proud of. Whatever your image of a fulfilled life looks like, the reality is your present circumstances may seem radically different.

It is easy to fall into the trap of discontent if you are not careful. You may have all the money and material things you can imagine and still feel lacking. Likewise, you may be enjoying a more modest life that gives you complete satisfaction. The difference has a lot to do with your viewpoint.

Your perspective is your reality. If you believe that material wealth alone will satisfy you then you may be trusting the wrong things to make you happy. Surrounding yourself with "stuff" is no guarantee of contentment. In most cases this results in extreme debt and frustration as you try to keep up with someone's lifestyle you crave.

The grass may look greener on the other side of the fence, but it still needs to be watered and mowed. The amount of time and energy you spend longing for someone else's life could be used to enjoy your own.

In addition, you have no idea who may be wishing for the life you want to escape from. You may be living someone else's dream. It is important to assess what you have in front of you and realize how blessed you are.

There is nothing wrong with wanting more out of life, especially if you are being mistreated, neglected, or lack basic human needs. But if your motives are rooted in greed or envy, then step back and evaluate your intentions.

Life is precious and short. Before you toss this one away, take a closer look. The life you always wanted might be the life you have right now; one you do not need to escape from but simply need to live.

Reflection for Today: What do you need to do to be satisfied with the life you have? Write down ways you can change your point of view.

Today's Affirmation: I will make a conscious effort to separate my wants from my needs. I will be glad for all that I have instead of focusing on what I do not. I will make the necessary adjustments in myself so I can determine if the life I have is enough.

NOTES:

CONTINUE TO GROW   ~ DAY 41 ~

Those who tried to bury you didn't realize you would continue to grow.

Obstacles are those frightful things you see when you take your eyes off your goal.

Henry Ford

Ada Lovelace lived in the 19th century and overcame immense opposition to become a trailblazer in the field of computing. Born in 1815, Lovelace was the daughter of the famous poet Lord Byron and mathematician Annabella Milbanke. Despite her aristocratic lineage, Ada's contributions to science and technology remain largely unrecognized.

Facing gender bias and restrictions, Lovelace fought against the prevailing belief that women were intellectually inferior. She displayed a remarkable aptitude for mathematics from an early age, due in part to her mother's insistence on her rigorous education. Lovelace's talent caught the attention of Charles Babbage, an English mathematician and inventor, who introduced her to his Analytical Engine. This was a precursor to modern day computers.

Her collaboration with Babbage resulted in Ada's most significant achievement: the publication of "Notes on the Analytical Engine" in 1843. In this groundbreaking work, Lovelace demonstrated her deep understanding of the potential of Babbage's machine. She not only explained its basic functions but also envisioned its capabilities beyond mere calculation. Her notes included the first-ever algorithm designed for a machine, making Ada Lovelace the world's first computer programmer.

Because of her incredible work, Ada is often referred to as the "Enchantress of Numbers." Her pioneering insights continue to inspire women in Science, Technology, Engineering, and Mathematics, (STEM), fields to this day.

The triumph of Ada Lovelace serves as a testament to the determination of those who dare to challenge societal norms. Her example reminds us that even the greatest opposition can be overcome. It also continues to encourage women to break barriers and build on their aspirations despite adversity.

Reflection for Today: Journal about how you can defeat a major hinderance or prejudice in your life to pursue a dream.

Today's Affirmation: I remind myself that no obstacle is too big, and no dream too lofty. I can achieve great things, just like those who have gone before me. I am fueled by their stories and am empowered to make a difference in the world.

NOTES:

<u>*OPEN YOUR EYES*</u>   *~ DAY 42 ~*

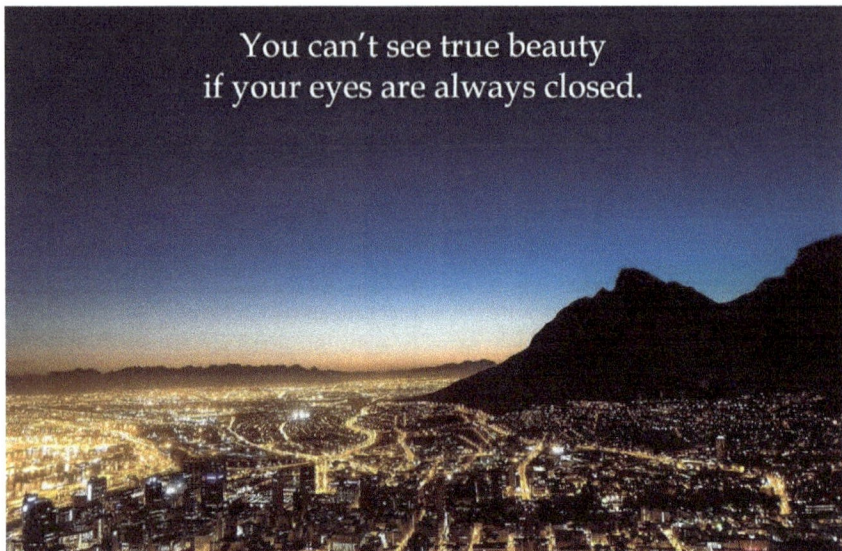

You can't see true beauty if your eyes are always closed.

I'm always angry about the death of people who are still alive.

Their eyes are open, yet they can't see anything.

Michael Bassey Johnson

Every year, Terry and I try to travel to Niagara Falls, Canada. We love the area and always schedule several stops during our time there. The most impressive, of course, is the trip to the falls themselves. They are breathtaking.

I remember the very first time we stood next to them. Thousands of gallons of water were rushing past us, and the roar was so loud we could hardly hear one another as mist swirled and rained down. We held each other with tear filled eyes in awestruck wonder. We were speechless.

The power of Niagara Falls creates an electricity in the air that is indescribable. It makes you feel very small and vulnerable...or at least it should.

After taking pictures and relishing the view, our eyes were opened to what else was in front of us. Just beyond the safety railing, all along the length of the water bank was discarded garbage. Paper cups, plastic bottles, and food wrappers were everywhere. Here we were at one of the most incredible wonders of the world and it was being treated like a trash can. Our hearts were broken.

Worst yet, the number of people who were simply stopping for a quick photo opportunity was disheartening. They seemed to have no sense of appreciation for this astounding landmark. I wish I could describe how sad this made us, but it is exactly how we can treat life in general.

We can become so wrapped up in day-to-day living that we forget to live and miss the beauty around us. Even worse, we can toss aside precious aspects of our lives without a second thought, such as careers, health, and companionship. Many times, we do not understand how important they are until it is too late.

We will still make our annual trips to see the majestic falls. We will also do our best to keep them fresh in our hearts each time. Though Niagara Falls may continue to flow and live on decades from now, we may not. Time is precious.

~Denise~

Reflection for Today: Write about a time you took something for granted that you wish you had today.

Today's Affirmation: I understand that life is short and that every moment is precious. I will do my best not to let familiarity steal my wonder. I will keep my eyes open and see beyond the day-to-day distractions of life.

NOTES:

A Better You in 45 Days

LEAVE A GOOD IMPRESSION   *~ DAY 43 ~*

Living a good life isn't about possessions, but the impressions you leave behind.

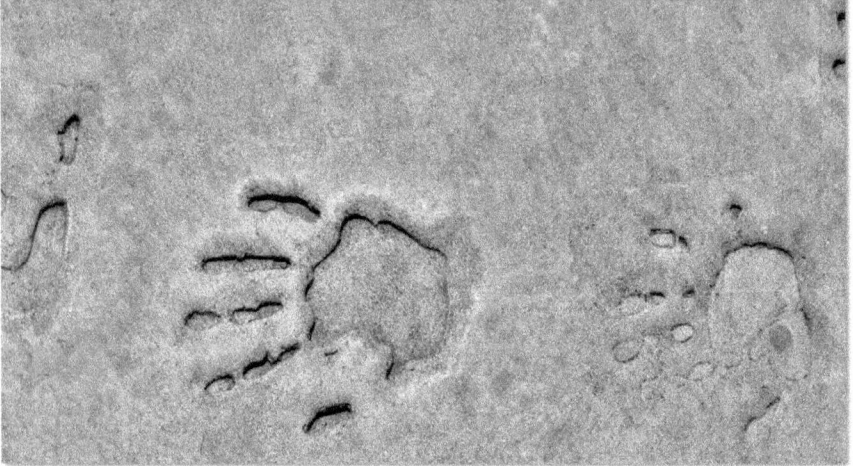

Living a good life isn't about possessions, but the impressions you leave behind.

We rise by lifting others.

Robert Ingersoll

In the realm of art, there are often unknown individuals who had a significant influence on the lives of famous artists. One such person is Theo van Gogh, the younger brother of the renowned Dutch painter Vincent van Gogh.

Theo van Gogh, born in 1857, played a pivotal role in encouraging his brother's artistic endeavors. As an art dealer and collector, Theo recognized Vincent's talent and provided unwavering emotional support. He was a sounding board, who also offered financial assistance and constructive feedback on Vincent's artwork.

Theo's impact on Vincent's life was profound. He introduced his brother to influential artists of the time. This included Paul Gauguin and Henri de Toulouse-Lautrec, expanding Vincent's artistic network. Theo also played a crucial role in promoting, exhibiting, and selling Vincent's paintings to a wider audience.

The brothers maintained a constant correspondence by exchanging letters. These not only detailed Vincent's artistic progress but helped calm him during periods of mental turmoil and doubt. Theo's steadfast belief in his brother's talent helped the artist endure personal and financial problems throughout his career.

Tragically, both brothers' lives were cut short. Vincent van Gogh died in 1890, and Theo, grief-stricken, passed away just six months later. However, Theo's efforts to promote Vincent's work continued after his death. Theo's widow Johanna van Gogh-Bonger played a crucial role in promoting van Gogh's art posthumously, preserving his legacy.

Today, Vincent van Gogh is celebrated as one of the most influential artists in history. This was only made possible by the support of the lesser-known brother, Theo. His example shows how one person's success can be fueled by another.

Reflection for Today: Think of ways you can help someone else live out their dreams and see success. Record your answer in the notes.

Denise and Terry Atkins

Today's Affirmation: I am grateful for the unseen influences that helped shape my life. I will strive to provide that same support to others by helping them fulfill their destinies with no expectation of reward.

NOTES:

DON'T LOOK BACK   ~ DAY 44 ~

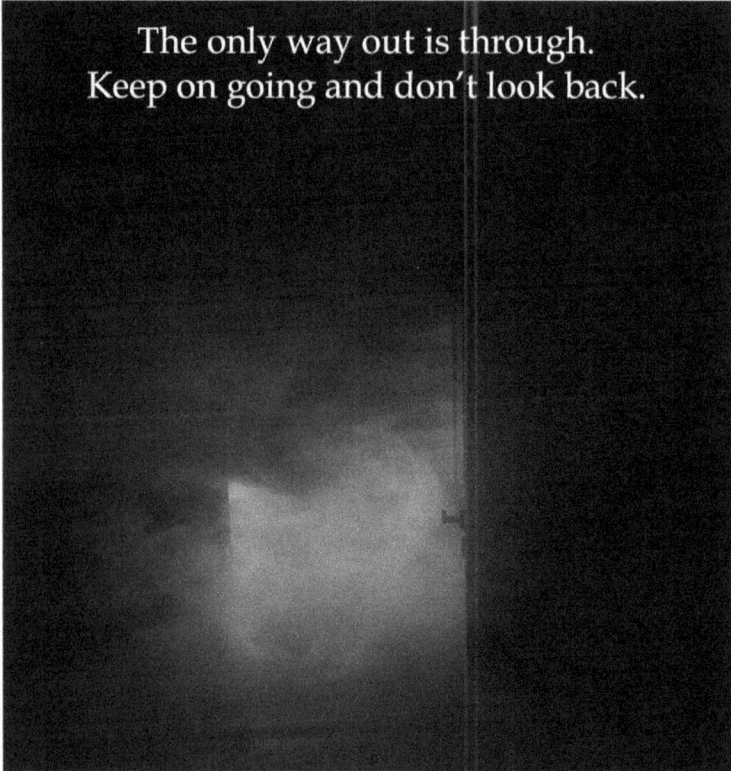

The only way out is through.
Keep on going and don't look back.

The only way out is through. Keep on going and don't look back.

Holding on is believing that there's only a past;

letting go is knowing that there's a future.

Daphne Rose Kingma

Alex always dreamed of participating in the annual Great Ocean Swim. This was a grueling 10-kilometer race that tested the endurance and stamina of swimmers from all over the world. With a heart full of ambition and hope, Alex trained relentlessly for the upcoming event.

On the day of the race, the sun spread wide and bright over the rolling waves. Swimmers lined up at the starting point in vibrant suits and caps. Among them stood Alex, ready to experience what lay ahead.

The whistle pierced the air, and the athletes dove into the ocean. Alex, fueled by determination, swam with all his might. Stroke after stroke, he pushed through the currents, matching the rhythm of the veteran swimmers beside him.

As the race progressed, however, fatigue began to take its toll on Alex's body. The once invigorating waves now felt like insurmountable barriers, and doubt crept into his mind. Alex was suddenly aware of the strain on his arms and legs. His breathing became more labored and the thought of turning back grew more tempting with every stroke. Perhaps it would be better to retreat and try again another day.

Reluctantly, Alex turned around with the weight of his decision settling in. The swimmers who passed by on their way to the finish line urged him to press on, but the powerful thoughts of giving up pulled him backwards on the course. With a heavy heart, Alex continued the long swim back to where the race began.

After what seemed like an eternity, he finally reached the sand and collapsed at the starting point, gasping heavily and exhausted. A young girl carefully approached him and asked why he turned back. "The waves were too great," he lamented, "I couldn't go on."

She looked at Alex sorrowfully and said, "But you were over halfway there. You should have kept going. By coming back, you swam longer than the length of the course."

Realization struck Alex like a crashing wave. Turning back only led to more work, more effort expended, and unbearable disappointment. The lesson became clear: by succumbing to doubt and choosing to retreat, Alex prolonged the journey.

Regardless of whether he won, completing the course would have been a personal victory for the young swimmer. Instead, he must start over some other time bearing the weight of this painful choice.

Like Alex, when you feel the urge to stop pursuing a dream or turn back, chances are you lose more than if you would have continued. Doubt and fear may come, especially when you are taking a chance on something new in your life. Ignore these feelings and keep your eyes on the goal.

Stand strong and remember how far you have come, and the time devoted to your progress. Do not allow anyone or anything to entice you to go back to where you started. Otherwise, your hard work will be for nothing.

Press through to the finish line into whatever adventures life has in store for you. Remember, you only fail when you stop trying.

Reflection for Today: Write about a dream you have given up on and how you can begin to pursue it.

Today's Affirmation: I will not be provoked into giving up my progress. I have come too far to turn back. The person I have become is too valuable to let go of. I will finish my race.

NOTES:

_____

_____

_____

_____

_____

_____

_____

_____

_____

_____

_____

A Better You in 45 Days

<u>DREAM ON</u>   ~ *DAY 45* ~

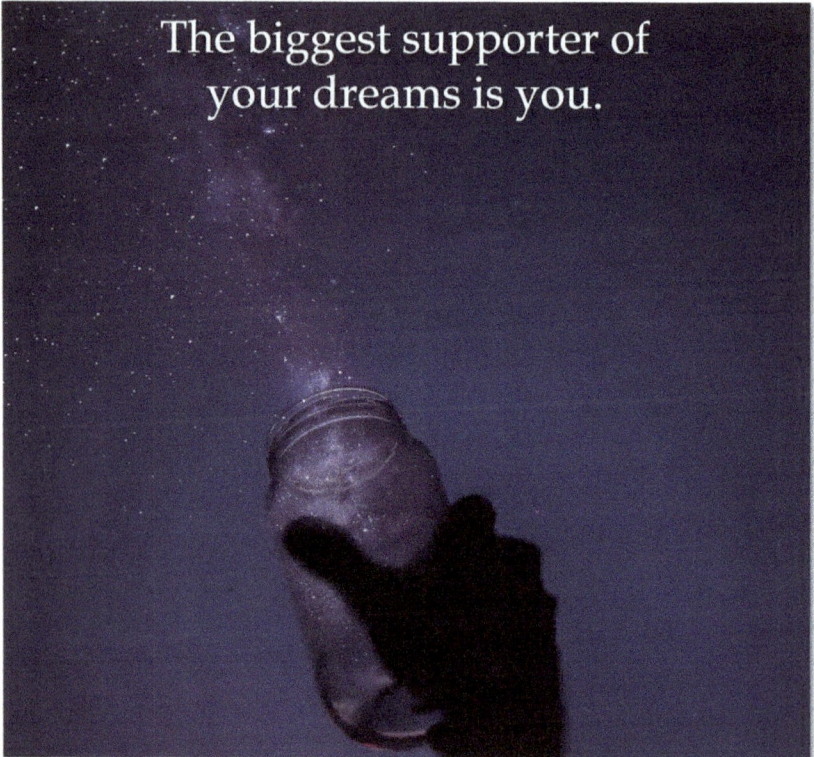

The biggest supporter of your dreams is you.

The best way to predict the future is to create it.

Peter Drucker

Congratulations! You have completed this forty-five-day challenge. Be proud of all you confronted and overcame, but do not let your efforts end here.

You dedicated a great deal of time and energy to introspection, allowing yourself to delve deep into your thoughts, emotions, and experiences. By engaging in regular journaling and reflective exercises, you created a sacred space for self-expression and awareness.

Keep going!

This book has only served as a guide and companion on your way to wellness. It provided you with prompts, exercises, and thought-provoking questions to aid your success. You have done the work and should feel good about all you accomplished.

As you move forward, it is important to carry the lessons and newfound wisdom with you. Continue to practice mindfulness habits. Embrace your new perspectives and use them to guide your decisions, actions, and goals.

Celebrate your achievements and the progress you made. It was not always easy, but your commitment and perseverance paid off. You showed great courage in facing your fears, exploring your vulnerabilities, and uncovering your strengths. Carry this with you throughout all aspects of your life.

Remember to be gentle with yourself. Allow room for mistakes, setbacks, and moments of uncertainty. Value the lessons learned and continue your work.

Congratulations, again, and thank you for allowing us to help you. We hope these pages inspired you to see yourself in a new light. The steps you took are brave and difficult. We are proud of you and wish you the best as you create a beautiful life.

~ Denise and Terry~

Reflection for Today: Look back over your previous reflection entries. In the notes section, write a summary of the progress you have made.

Today's Affirmation: I am proud of myself for completing this forty-five-day personal reflection. I showed dedication and commitment to my own growth. I will be kind to myself, remembering that life comes in stages.

I look forward to the whole and healthy person I am becoming. I am excited to pursue my dreams with an open mind and believe I have what it takes to make them reality. The possibilities that await me are endless.

NOTES:

Denise and Terry Atkins

———— ∞ ————

POSTFACE

Life can be hard.

Our primary family unit is relatively small compared to most. It consists of our two adult children, their families, and our nine-year old golden retrievers, Marley, and Daisy. Both dogs were born two days apart from the same father and different mothers. They were raised by Denise from puppies and were inseparable. The pair was a source of great support for her, especially during her previous husband's years-long battle with cancer. They also openly loved their Papa Terry as soon as he became a part of their family.

As we were closing in on the final edits of this book, we noticed that Marley, a beautiful red male, began to limp after a slip on the stairs leading to our back yard. We didn't think much of it at first but became more concerned when the limp grew progressively worse over a period of weeks. One day, on his way outside for his morning exercise with his sister, Marley slipped on our kitchen floor and needed Terry's assistance to stand. At that moment we knew something significant was happening concerning his health. We called a nearby 24-hour animal hospital and took him in for an appointment later that day.

Marley patiently allowed the techs and doctor to pull, poke and examine him with no indication of pain. The team drew bloodwork and performed an x-ray on his leg to better determine the issue. The doctor's initial thoughts were that our fur baby had Lyme Disease or perhaps a small fracture or tear that was causing him to limp. We sat quietly as he left us with Marley to examine the results of the tests. Our world stopped for a moment when he returned.

The x-ray showed that Marley had Osteosarcoma (OSA) in his right leg above the knee. This is the most common type of cancerous bone tumor in dogs and spreads aggressively. Once diagnosed, 80 percent of dogs with OSA die within four months due to lung metastasis. The only treatment options available to us were amputation of the limb or euthanasia. Marley was a large dog and because of his size, and age, amputation would have been extremely taxing on his body. There were no guarantees that all the cancer would be removed, and if any of the microscopic cells had already reached his lungs, we would only be prolonging the inevitable. So, with tears of anguish we made the decision that was best for our beloved companion. We said goodbye.

The clinic took Denise and Marley to a comfort room with low lighting, a couch, and snacks. Terry went home to bring Daisy for one last moment with her brother. While Terry was away, Denise lay beside Marley gently petting his head. Tearfully she expressed her love and appreciation for him being such a great dog through the years. When the pair returned, Daisy ran excitedly to Marley, licking him and nudging him to play. Terry sat on the couch, lifting Marley's face, and telling him repeatedly that he was a good boy. Daisy settled down beside Marley who placed his head against Terry's leg and rested against Denise for the last time. Our small family spent the final moments with him waiting for the end to come.

The doctor was gentle and caring. The procedure was quick and painless. Quietly, with his head in Denise's arms, his family hugging him and whispering their love into his ears, Marley left this earth.

In our introduction, we shared that we are not writing as spectators, but participants, in life's heartaches. Losing Marley so suddenly was a shock, but we can honestly say we treasured every moment with him. There are no "should haves" concerning how we expressed love to our boy every day. He had a full life, and we did our best to cherish the moments together and show our gratitude.

The night before Marley left us, Denise danced with him and his sister while we cooked dinner. Marley did his best to keep up even though he could not put much weight on his back leg. That same evening, Terry sat on the floor with him gently trying to figure out what was happening to Marley's leg. In a show of affection, Marley rested his paw on Terry's arm.

Denise and Terry Atkins

Terry looked into his eyes and told Marley several times that he was a good boy. We both expressed our love for Marley that entire day, (as we did in many ways every day), not knowing that those moments would be some of our last with him. We have no regrets.

Making the decision to say goodbye to Marley was heart-wrenching, but it was a choice based solely on our love for him. Though it would have been easier on us emotionally to put him through the surgeries, chemo treatments, and prolonged recovery, we did what was best for him, not us. That is what sacrificial love looks like. We did not want his last memories to be filled with more pain and a reduced quality of life. Instead, he went into eternity as the active and playful dog he always was.

Throughout this book, we stressed the importance of valuing those who make a difference in your life. It is crucial to hold every moment with your loved ones close to your heart, because you never know when those moments will end. None of us is promised tomorrow and the life you have today can change in an instant. The worst thing that can happen is knowing you could have loved someone better and will never have the chance again. Take nothing for granted.

How will our family get through this loss? The same way we expressed in so many articles of this book. We will take each day as it comes. We will give ourselves the time and space we need to grieve. We will reflect on our beautiful memories of Marley and comfort Daisy through her pain and loneliness as best we can. Above all, we will lean on each other through this season of sadness until we can see the light again.

We will miss you every day, Marley, (aka Mars Bars, aka Marls Barkley). You were such a good boy and a great companion. Everyone you met fell in love with you. You will forever be in our hearts.

We love you, buddy!

In Loving
Memory

Marley Atkins

December 4, 2014
to
January 29, 2024

CHT Promo and Coupon Page

Denise and Terry Atkins are high school friends, and now husband and wife. They have certifications in Happiness Life Coaching, Meditation and Wellness, and Cognitive-Behavioral Therapy. Together they launched the wellness platform, "Create Happiness Today". This site features information, podcasts, blogs and more to help others find happiness that is well within reach.

CHT was originally created as a haven for people suffering loss because of death, illness, divorce, or estrangement. Denise and Terry soon realized they were spending much of their time speaking to others about the various aspects of love, life, and relationships. Naturally, the couple felt compelled to broaden their focus and are now ambassadors of change and self-improvement in a world that sorely needs it.

As a thank you for purchasing this book, they are offering you a **20% off coupon** for your next order at their merchandise store.

https://www.merchcreatehappinesstoday.com/

Use the code **45DaysBetter** at checkout to receive your discount.

Follow **Denise and Terry Atkins** at the links below to stay connected and find new ways to **Live Well, Love Deeply, and Laugh Often.**

Website: https://createhappinesstoday.com

Podcast: https://open.spotify.com/show/5RPFnof0OHct3efiPcNSYZ

Facebook: https://www.facebook.com/CHT.CreateHappinessToday/

Twitter: https://twitter.com/CHT_Tweets

Instagram: https://www.instagram.com/cht.createhappinesstoday/

LinkedIn: https://www.linkedin.com/company/cht-createhappinesstoday

Email: contact@createhappinesstoday.com

Denise and Terry Atkins

The best view is on the other side of the mountain.

~Create Happiness Today~

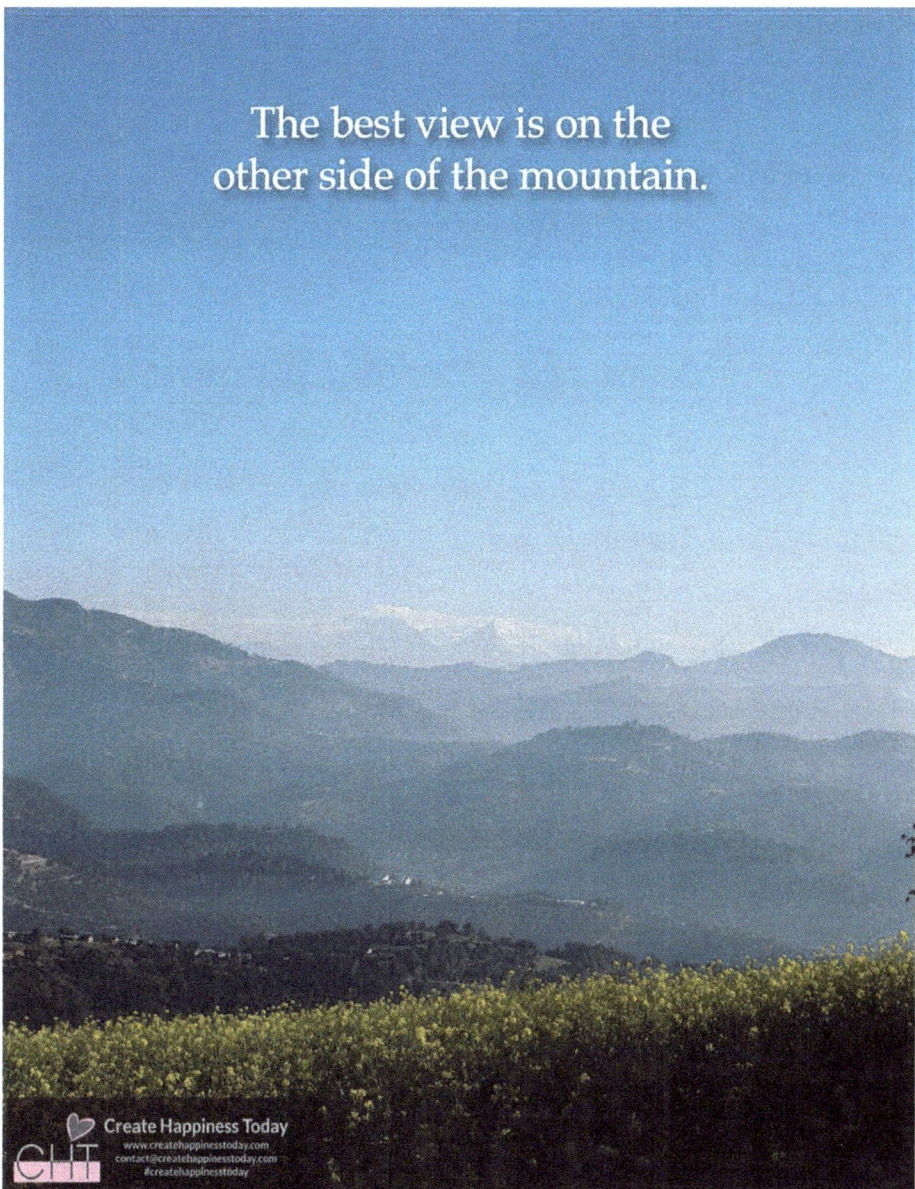

The best view is on the other side of the mountain.

Create Happiness Today
www.createhappinesstoday.com
contact@createhappinesstoday.com
#createhappinesstoday

www.ingramcontent.com/pod-product-compliance
Lightning Source LLC
Chambersburg PA
CBHW062101080426
42734CB00012B/2713